# DUINESIAN ELEGIES

UNIVERSITY OF NORTH CAROLINA
STUDIES IN THE GERMANIC LANGUAGES
AND LITERATURES

*Initiated by* RICHARD JENTE (1949–1952), *established by* F. E. COENEN (1952–1968)

*Publication Committee*

SIEGFRIED MEWS, EDITOR   JOHN G. KUNSTMANN   GEORGE S. LANE

HERBERT W. REICHERT   CHRISTOPH E. SCHWEITZER   SIDNEY R. SMITH

70. Donald F. Nelson. PORTRAIT OF THE ARTIST AS HERMES. A Study of Myth and Psychology in Thomas Mann's *Felix Krull*. 1971. Pp. xvi, 160. $6.75.

71. Murray A. and Marian L. Cowie, eds. THE WORKS OF PETER SCHOTT (1460–1490). Vol. II: Commentary. 1971. Pp. xxix, 534. Cloth $14.50; Paper $13.00.

72. Christine Oertel Sjögren. THE MARBLE STATUE AS IDEA: COLLECTED ESSAYS ON ADALBERT STIFTER'S *DER NACHSOMMER*. 1972. Pp. xiv, 121. Cloth $7.00.

73. Donald G. Daviau and Jorun B. Johns, eds. THE CORRESPONDENCE OF ARTHUR SCHNITZLER AND RAOUL AUERHEIMER WITH RAOUL AUERNHEIMER'S APHORISMS. 1972. Pp. xii, 161. Cloth $7.50.

74. A. Margaret Arent Madelung. THE LAXDOELA SAGA: ITS STRUCTURAL PATTERNS. 1972. Pp. xiv, 261. Cloth $9.25.

75. Jeffrey L. Sammons. SIX ESSAYS ON THE YOUNG GERMAN NOVEL. 1972. Pp. xiv, 187. Cloth $7.75.

76. Donald H. Crosby and George C. Schoolfield, eds. STUDIES IN THE GERMAN DRAMA. A *FESTSCHRIFT* IN HONOR OF WALTER SILZ. 1974. Pp. xxvi, 255. Cloth $10.75.

77. J. W. Thomas. TANNHÄUSER: POET AND LEGEND. With Texts and Translations of his Works. 1974. Pp. x, 202. Cloth $10.75.

78. Olga Marx and Ernst Morwitz, trans. THE WORKS OF STEFAN GEORGE. 1974. 2nd, rev. and enl. ed. Pp. xxviii, 431. Cloth $12.90.

79. Siegfried Mews and Herbert Knust, eds. ESSAYS ON BRECHT: THEATER AND POLITICS. 1974. Pp. xiv, 241. Cloth $11.95.

80. Donald G. Daviau and George J. Buelow. THE *ARIADNE AUF NAXOS* OF HUGO VON HOFMANNSTHAL AND RICHARD STRAUSS. 1975. Pp. x, 274. Cloth $12.75.

81. Elaine E. Boney. RAINER MARIA RILKE: *DUINESIAN ELEGIES*. German Text with English Translation and Commentary. 1975. Pp. xii, 153. Cloth $10.75.

*For other volumes in the "Studies" see pages 151 ff.*

Send orders to: (U.S. and Canada)
The University of North Carolina Press, P.O. Box 2288
Chapel Hill, N.C. 27514
(All other countries) Feffer and Simons, Inc., 31 Union Square, New York, N.Y. 10003

NUMBER EIGHTY-ONE


UNIVERSITY
OF NORTH CAROLINA
STUDIES IN
THE GERMANIC LANGUAGES
AND LITERATURES

Karl Hittmann

# RAINER MARIA RILKE

## *Duinesian Elegies*

German Text

with

English Translation and Commentary

by

Elaine E. Boney

CHAPEL HILL

THE UNIVERSITY OF NORTH CAROLINA PRESS

1975

**Library of Congress Cataloging in Publication Data**

Rilke, Rainer Maria, 1875–1926.
  Duinesian elegies.

  (University of North Carolina studies in the Germanic languages and literatures, no. 81)

  I. Boney, Elaine Emesette, 1921–   . II. Title. III. Series: North Carolina. University. Studies in the Germanic languages and literatures, no. 81.
PT2635.I65D8 1975          831'.9'12          74-16015
ISBN O-8078-8081-7

Manufactured in the U.S.A.

# CONTENTS

# FOREWORD

My study of the *Duineser Elegien* began with a seminar under Professor Robert T. Clarke, Jr. at the University of Texas, continued through a year of study under Professor Steffen Steffensen at the University of Copenhagen, and produced my dissertation, "Existentialist Thought in the Works of Rainer Maria Rilke" (University of Texas, 1958), which was completed under the supervision of Professor Helmut Rehder. Although I long have been aware of the need for a better translation of the Elegies, I hesitated to attempt a translation myself, for I knew that I could not do justice to the great beauty of the original. Nevertheless, like Malte in Rilke's novel, *Die Aufzeichnungen des Malte Laurids Brigge,* I found that this was a task which had to be undertaken. When the translation was completed, it was obvious that a good interpretation was needed to accompany it since the only extensive critical treatment of the Elegies available in English is *Rilke's Duino Elegies: An Interpretation* (1961), a translation of *Rainer Maria Rilkes Deutung des Daseins* by Romano Guardini. It also became clear that some of Rilke's letters relating to the Elegies were needed to complete this volume.

An examination of the translations now in print has confirmed my general impression of need for a new one. Since the completion of my own rendering a version by Stephen Garmey and Jay Wilson has appeared. Of the three translations presently in print this one was lyrically the most promising despite some errors resulting from inadequate knowledge of the German language and others caused by insufficient understanding of Rilke's thought. These authors have relied on the Spender–Leishman translation in their resolution of the major problems of translation for which I have attempted to find new solutions.

The remaining translations are by English writers and thus are attuned to the British more than to the American idiom and style. The Spender–Leishman translation, which appeared in 1939, is a great achievement. It has made the Elegies available in English for many years while there was no other adequate edition. Although it is still the best known and most widely used English version of the Elegies, major research on the Elegies has appeared since that time which contributes to a more complete understanding of them than was possible in 1939.

Of the existing translations the rhythmic version by C. F. MacIntyre is the most accurate. As a scholar of German literature, MacIntyre was familiar with the important critical literature, and his understanding of the Elegies is mirrored in his translation. In contrast to MacIntyre, I opted for freedom with regard to rhythmic patterns, and thus I have greater latitude in choice of words while retaining a lyrical quality.

Translation must grow from understanding of a work beyond mere comprehension of language. My own work with Rilke has been existentially oriented with the view of man as an imperfect, limited being necessarily imprisoned in his own world as a central and basic concept. These limitations fragment man's view of the world, for from his position within the whole he never can view totality as an object, a whole. He is caught between the creature world with an innate harmony which he himself has lost and his intuitive awareness of the angel world of the absolute—an awareness which is painful because he can only sense but never know it. Given these limitations, man must question the meaning of human life, a meaning which Rilke ultimately finds in man's position in the middle. Through the inner world of his heart man transforms physical reality into an intangible form which the angel can comprehend, while at the same time he rescues transitory reality into the permanence of the angel world. From his position in the middle he relates to each other these two worlds, which otherwise would remain separate; in this manner he acquires his unique responsibility, meaning, and task within the universe as a function of his singular nature. The elegies thus are tightly structured around a pattern of separation imposed upon man by the fact of his corporeity, a separation which is not only a painful limitation but also the source of his hope and significance. Life, together with its ultimate limitation of death, can be affirmed as a necessary and meaningful state within a meaningful whole wherein man does not perish but undergoes transformation.

In making this translation I have considered meaning—even to the point of trying to retain layers of meaning—the highest value. Beyond ascertaining meaning, I have tried to formulate it in clear, poetically cadenced English in an effort to capture a shadow of the original beauty. I have made no effort to retain the original meter, and where the original meter is preserved, it happens by chance. I have sought to translate not merely the words of the elegies, but also their essence—to re-create this work in good, clear English. Basically untranslatable expressions have been stated as equivalent thoughts rather than words, and certain choices had to be made. Although some readers will disagree with my choices, they were made with careful deliberation and represent the best decisions that I could reach.

During the years of my concern with Rilke's works I have received help and encouragement from many sources. The late Professor Robert T. Clarke's seminar on Rilke at the University of Texas in 1948 was responsible for my decision to write my dissertation on Rilke, and subsequent study with Professor Steffen Steffensen and Professor Helmut Rehder developed the critical judgment necessary for scholarly endeavor. I am especially grateful to Professor Robert M. Browning of Hamilton College for his many valuable suggestions concerning stylistic nuances, interpretation, and occasional errors, for they greatly improved the accuracy and poetic quality of the translation. My colleague, Professor Harvey I. Dunkle, has been very helpful in solving some of the most difficult linguistic problems, and Professor Allan W. Anderson has suggested improvements in philosophical terminology in the commentary. Professor Ernest Wolf and Professor Guenther C. Rimbach read portions of the manuscript and provided me with early encouragement. Professor Mary Redding assisted me with writing the foreword, the most difficult portion of this work to formulate. Professor Suzanne Henig gave my work its first public exposure by publishing selections from the translation in the first issue of the *Virginia Woolf Quarterly* (Fall 1972). Our departmental secretaries, Mrs. Viola M. Beatty and Miss Alice J. Clary, have contributed countless hours of typing. To all who have given me help and encouragement I gratefully acknowledge my indebtedness. Most of all I am grateful to Rainer Maria Rilke for giving the world this incomparably beautiful work which has been my companion for so many years.

W. W. Norton & Co. has graciously granted permission for use of the German text from Rilke's *Sämtliche Werke* I (Frankurt am Main: Insel, 1955). Without the German text this edition of my translation would have been hopelessly incomplete since no translation can adequately replace the original. Norton's permission is most gratefully acknowledged. The permission of Insel Verlag to publish the translations of the three letters in the appendices makes their inclusion possible and is acknowledged with pleasure.

Special acknowledgment is due Professor Karl Hittmann of Salzburg, Austria, for permission to use his original block print of the angel in this edition. Professor Hittmann, a graduate of the Vienna Art Academy, is a professional artist whose work I have long admired. In his design rays form an angel of light with circles conveying a sense of the cosmic. The abstractness of the artist's design provides a visual parallel to the abstractness of the Rilke angel.

Elaine E. Boney   30 May 1974

# DUINESER ELEGIEN—DUINESIAN ELEGIES

# DIE ERSTE ELEGIE

Wer, wenn ich schriee, hörte mich denn aus der Engel
Ordnungen? und gesetzt selbst, es nähme
einer mich plötzlich ans Herz: ich verginge von seinem
stärkeren Dasein. Denn das Schöne ist nichts
5   als des Schrecklichen Anfang, den wir noch grade ertragen,
und wir bewundern es so, weil es gelassen verschmäht,
uns zu zerstören. Ein jeder Engel ist schrecklich.
    Und so verhalt ich mich denn und verschlucke den Lockruf
dunkelen Schluchzens. Ach, wen vermögen
10   wir denn zu brauchen? Engel nicht, Menschen nicht,
und die findigen Tiere merken es schon,
daß wir nicht sehr verläßlich zu Haus sind
in der gedeuteten Welt. Es bleibt uns vielleicht
irgend ein Baum an dem Abhang, daß wir ihn täglich
15   wiedersähen; es bleibt uns die Straße von gestern
und das verzogene Treusein einer Gewohnheit,
der es bei uns gefiel, und so blieb sie und ging nicht.
    O und die Nacht, die Nacht, wenn der Wind voller Weltraum
uns am Angesicht zehrt—, wem bliebe sie nicht, die ersehnte,
20   sanft enttäuschende, welche dem einzelnen Herzen
mühsam bevorsteht. Ist sie den Liebenden leichter?
Ach, sie verdecken sich nur mit einander ihr Los.
    Weißt du's *noch* nicht? Wirf aus den Armen die Leere
zu den Räumen hinzu, die wir atmen; vielleicht daß die Vögel
25   die erweiterte Luft fühlen mit innigerm Flug.


Ja, die Frühlinge brauchten dich wohl. Es muteten manche
Sterne dir zu, daß du sie spürtest. Es hob
sich eine Woge heran im Vergangenen, oder
da du vorüberkamst am geöffneten Fenster,
30   gab eine Geige sich hin. Das alles war Auftrag.
Aber bewältigtest du's? Warst du nicht immer
noch von Erwartung zerstreut, als kündigte alles
eine Geliebte dir an? (Wo willst du sie bergen,

2

# THE FIRST ELEGY

Who of the angelic hosts would hear me, even if I
cried out? Yet granted, one of them suddenly
embraced me, I would only perish from his
stronger being. For beauty is nothing but
5    the beginning of awesomeness which we can barely endure
and we marvel at it so because it calmly disdains
to destroy us. Each and every angel is awesome.
    And so I restrain myself and suppress the luring call
with somber sobs. Oh, who can possibly be of
10   use to us? Neither men nor angels,
and the clever animals have already marked
that we are not very securely at home
in our conceptualized world. Perhaps there is left for us
some tree on a slope that we might see it every day;
15   there remains for us yesterday's road
and the pampered fidelity of a habit
which was comfortable with us, and so it remained and did not go
        away.
    O, and the night, the night when wind filled with space
feeds on our faces—, for whom would it not remain, the longed-for,
20   gently undeceiving night, which painfully challenges
the lonely heart? Is it easier for lovers?
Alas, they only conceal their lot by each other.
    You *still* do not understand? Cast the emptiness from your arms
into the space that we breathe; possibly the birds
25   can sense the expanded air with more intense flight.

Yes, the springtimes truly had need of you. Many a star reached
out for you to notice it. A wave
commenced somewhere in the past, or
when you went by an open window
30   a violin sang out. All that was your responsibility.
But did you measure up to it? Were you not always distracted
by expectations, as if everything spoke to you
of a loved one? (Where do you plan to shelter her,

da doch die großen fremden Gedanken bei dir
35  aus und ein gehn und öfters bleiben bei Nacht.)
Sehnt es dich aber, so singe die Liebenden; lange
noch nicht unsterblich genug ist ihr berühmtes Gefühl.
Jene, du neidest sie fast, Verlassenen, die du
so viel liebender fandst als die Gestillten. Beginn
40  immer von neuem die nie zu erreichende Preisung;
denk: es erhält sich der Held, selbst der Untergang war ihm
nur ein Vorwand, zu sein: seine letzte Geburt.
Aber die Liebenden nimmt die erschöpfte Natur
in sich zurück, als wären nicht zweimal die Kräfte,
45  dieses zu leisten. Hast du der Gaspara Stampa
denn genügend gedacht, daß irgend ein Mädchen,
dem der Geliebte entging, am gesteigerten Beispiel
dieser Liebenden fühlt: daß ich würde wie sie?
Sollen nicht endlich uns diese ältesten Schmerzen
50  fruchtbarer werden? Ist es nicht Zeit, daß wir liebend
uns vom Geliebten befrein und es bebend bestehn:
wie der Pfeil die Sehne besteht, um gesammelt im Absprung
*mehr* zu sein als er selbst. Denn Bleiben ist nirgends.

Stimmen, Stimmen. Höre, mein Herz, wie sonst nur
55  Heilige hörten: daß sie der riesige Ruf
aufhob vom Boden; sie aber knieten,
Unmögliche, weiter und achtetens nicht:
*So* waren sie hörend. Nicht, daß du *Gottes* ertrügest
die Stimme, bei weitem. Aber das Wehende höre,
60  die ununterbrochene Nachricht, die aus Stille sich bildet.
Es rauscht jetzt von jenen jungen Toten zu dir.
Wo immer du eintratst, redete nicht in Kirchen
zu Rom und Neapel ruhig ihr Schicksal dich an?
Oder es trug eine Inschrift sich erhaben dir auf,
65  wie neulich die Tafel in Santa Maria Formosa.
Was sie mir wollen? leise soll ich des Unrechts
Anschein abtun, der ihrer Geister
reine Bewegung manchmal ein wenig behindert.

Freilich ist es seltsam, die Erde nicht mehr zu bewohnen,
70  kaum erlernte Gebräuche nicht mehr zu üben,
Rosen, und andern eigens versprechenden Dingen

4

since the great strange thoughts come and go
35 in your mind and sometimes stay at night.)
If you feel such a longing, however, then sing of lovers; their
renowned feeling is far from immortal enough.
Those rejected lovers, you almost envy them, whom you
found so much more loving than the fulfilled ones. Begin
40 over and over again the never attainable praising;
consider: the hero lives on, even death was for him
merely a pretext for being: his ultimate birth.
But exhausted nature receives those who love
back to itself anew, as if there were not enough strength
45 to accomplish this once again.    Have you considered sufficiently
Gaspara Stampa, that some girl
left behind by her beloved might learn
from her exalted example to become like her?
Should not these primordial sorrows finally become
50 more productive for us? Is it not time for us lovingly
to free ourselves from the loved one and tremblingly endure:
as the arrow endures the bowstring so that concentrated in release
it is *more* than itself. For nowhere is there permanence.

Voices, voices. Listen my heart, as once only
55 holy men listened, so that the overwhelming summons
raised them up from the ground; they, impossible ones,
continued to kneel and did not even notice; they were
listeners like *that*. Not that you could possibly endure
*God's* voice. But listen to the indefinable wafting,
60 the never-ending message formed of silence.
A rustling comes to you now from those who died young.
Did not their fate speak quietly to you wherever
you entered in churches in Rome and in Naples?
Or an inscription obligated you nobly
65 as recently the tablet in Santa Maria Formosa.
What do they want of me? gently I am to remove
the aura of injustice which sometimes slightly
hinders the pure motion of their spirits.

To be sure, it is strange no longer to live on earth,
70 no longer to practice the customs barely learned there,
not to give roses and other intentionally expressive objects

5

nicht die Bedeutung menschlicher Zukunft zu geben;
das, was man war in unendlich ängstlichen Händen,
nicht mehr zu sein, und selbst den eigenen Namen
75   wegzulassen wie ein zerbrochenes Spielzeug.
Seltsam, die Wünsche nicht weiterzuwünschen. Seltsam,
alles, was sich bezog, so lose im Raume
flattern zu sehen. Und das Totsein ist mühsam
und voller Nachholn, daß man allmählich ein wenig
80   Ewigkeit spürt.—Aber Lebendige machen
alle den Fehler, daß sie zu stark unterscheiden.
Engel (sagt man) wüßten oft nicht, ob sie unter
Lebenden gehn oder Toten. Die ewige Strömung
reißt durch beide Bereiche alle Alter
85   immer mit sich und übertönt sie in beiden.

Schließlich brauchen sie uns nicht mehr, die Früheentrückten,
man entwöhnt sich des Irdischen sanft, wie man den Brüsten
milde der Mutter entwächst. Aber wir, die so große
Geheimnisse brauchen, denen aus Trauer so oft
90   seliger Fortschritt entspringt—: *könnten* wir sein ohne sie?
Ist die Sage umsonst, daß einst in der Klage um Linos
wagende erste Musik dürre Erstarrung durchdrang;
daß erst im erschrockenen Raum, dem ein beinah göttlicher
     Jüngling
plötzlich für immer enttrat, das Leere in jene
95   Schwingung geriet, die uns jetzt hinreißt und tröstet und hilft.

the meaning of human futurity;
no longer to be that which one was in infinitely
anxious hands, and even to leave behind
75   one's very name like a worn out toy.
Strange not to continue making wishes. Strange
to see everything that related floating
so freely in space. And being dead is wearisome
and full of catching up before one gradually senses
80   a little eternity.—But the living all
make the mistake of distinguishing too sharply.
Angels (they say) often do not know whether they
are among the living or the dead. The eternal
current ever bears all ages along through
85   both realms and drowns them out in both.

In the end they no longer need us, those youthfully dead,
one gently outgrows the earthly sphere, as one tenderly
outgrows the breasts of the mother. But we who have need
of great mysteries, for whom blessed growth often springs
90   from great sorrow—: *could* we exist without them?
Is the legend in vain, that once in the mourning for Linos
earliest tentative music broke through arid benumbment;
that in the startled space, which a nearly godlike youth
suddenly left forever, there first began in the emptiness
95   those vibrations which now enrapture and comfort and help us.

7

# DIE ZWEITE ELEGIE

Jeder Engel ist schrecklich. Und dennoch, weh mir,
ansing ich euch, fast tödliche Vögel der Seele,
wissend um euch. Wohin sind die Tage Tobiae,
da der Strahlendsten einer stand an der einfachen Haustür,
     5  zur Reise ein wenig verkleidet und schon nicht mehr furchtbar;
(Jüngling dem Jüngling, wie er neugierig hinaussah).
Träte der Erzengel jetzt, der gefährliche, hinter den Sternen
eines Schrittes nur nieder und herwärts: hochauf—
schlagend erschlüg uns das eigene Herz. Wer seid ihr?

 10  Frühe Geglückte, ihr Verwöhnten der Schöpfung,
Höhenzüge, morgenrötliche Grate
aller Erschaffung,—Pollen der blühenden Gottheit,
Gelenke des Lichtes, Gänge, Treppen, Throne,
Räume aus Wesen, Schilde aus Wonne, Tumulte
 15  stürmisch entzückten Gefühls und plötzlich, einzeln,
*Spiegel*: die die entströmte eigene Schönheit
wiederschöpfen zurück in das eigene Antlitz.

Denn wir, wo wir fühlen, verflüchtigen; ach wir
atmen uns aus und dahin; von Holzglut zu Holzglut
 20  geben wir schwächern Geruch. Da sagt uns wohl einer:
ja, du gehst mir ins Blut, dieses Zimmer, der Frühling
füllt sich mit dir ... Was hilfts, er kann uns nicht halten,
wir schwinden in ihm und um ihn. Und jene, die schön sind,
o wer hält sie zurück? Unaufhörlich steht Anschein
 25  auf in ihrem Gesicht und geht fort. Wie Tau von dem Frühgras
hebt sich das Unsre von uns, wie die Hitze von einem
heißen Gericht. O Lächeln, wohin? O Aufschaun:
neue, warme, entgehende Welle des Herzens—;
weh mir: wir *sinds* doch. Schmeckt denn der Weltraum,
 30  in den wir uns lösen, nach uns? Fangen die Engel
wirklich nur Ihriges auf, ihnen Entströmtes,
oder ist manchmal, wie aus Versehen, ein wenig
unseres Wesens dabei? Sind wir in ihre

# THE SECOND ELEGY

Every angel is awesome. Yet, alas, I still
sing to you, near fatal birds of the soul,
knowing of you. Where are the days of Tobias,
when one of the brightest angels stood at a simple threshold,
5  slightly disguised for the journey and no longer fearsome;
(a youth to the youth when he looked out curiously).
Now, if from beyond the stars the archangel, perilous to us,
were to approach just one step nearer, leaping
upward, our own hearts would slay us. Who are you?

10  Sucessful first creatures, favorites of creation,
high mountain ranges, dawn-reddened peaks
of all creation, pollen of the flowering Godhead,
junctures of light, avenues, stairways, thrones,
spaces of essence, shields of ecstasy, storms
15  of tumultuously enraptured emotion and suddenly, singly,
*mirrors* which reconcentrate once again in their
countenances their own outflowing beauty.

For we, when we are stirred, evanesce, we
breathe our lives out and away; from ember to glowing ember
20  we give off a fainter odor. Of course there are those
who say, you get in my blood, this room, the springtime
is filled with you . . . But what does it matter? They cannot sustain
    us,
we perish in and around them. And those who are lovely,
o, who can hold them back? Appearance continually comes
25  and goes on their faces. Like dew from the morning grass
that which is ours forsakes us, like heat
from hot food. Whither, o smile? O upward glance:
new warm wave escaping from the heart—;
but, alas, that is how we *are*. Does the space
30  into which we fade taste of us? Do the angels gather in
only what has radiated from them,
or is there sometimes by accident some of our substance
with it? Are there traces of us in their features,

Züge soviel nur gemischt wie das Vage in die Gesichter
35  schwangerer Frauen? Sie merken es nicht in dem Wirbel
ihrer Rückkehr zu sich. (Wie sollten sie's merken.)

Liebende könnten, verstünden sie's, in der Nachtluft
wunderlich reden. Denn es scheint, daß uns alles
verheimlicht. Siehe, die Bäume *sind;* die Häuser,
40  die wir bewohnen, bestehn noch. Wir nur
ziehen allem vorbei wie ein luftiger Austausch.
Und alles ist einig, uns zu verschweigen, halb als
Schande vielleicht und halb als unsägliche Hoffnung.
  Liebende, euch, ihr in einander Genügten,
45  frag ich nach uns. Ihr greift euch. Habt ihr Beweise?
Seht, mir geschiehts, daß meine Hände einander
inne werden oder daß mein gebrauchtes
Gesicht in ihnen sich schont. Das giebt mir ein wenig
Empfindung. Doch wer wagte darum schon zu *sein?*
50  Ihr aber, die ihr im Entzücken des anderen
zunehmt, bis er euch überwältigt
anfleht: nicht *mehr*—; die ihr unter den Händen
euch reichlicher werdet wie Traubenjahre;
die ihr manchmal vergeht, nur weil der andre
55  ganz überhand nimmt: euch frag ich nach uns. Ich weiß,
ihr berührt euch so selig, weil die Liebkosung verhält,
weil die Stelle nicht schwindet, die ihr, Zärtliche,
zudeckt; weil ihr darunter das reine
Dauern verspürt. So versprecht ihr euch Ewigkeit fast
60  von der Umarmung. Und doch, wenn ihr der ersten
Blicke Schrecken besteht und die Sehnsucht am Fenster,
und den ersten gemeinsamen Gang, *ein* Mal durch den Garten:
Liebende, *seid* ihrs dann noch? Wenn ihr einer dem andern
euch an den Mund hebt und ansetzt—: Getränk an Getränk:
65  o wie entgeht dann der Trinkende seltsam der Handlung.

Erstaunte euch nicht auf attischen Stelen die Vorsicht
menschlicher Geste? war nicht Liebe und Abschied
so leicht auf die Schultern gelegt, als wär es aus anderm
Stoffe gemacht als bei uns? Gedenkt euch der Hände,
70  wie sie drucklos beruhen, obwohl in den Torsen die Kraft steht.

mixed in like vagueness in the faces of
35  pregnant women? They do not take note of it in the whirlwind
of their return to themselves. (How could they perceive it.)

Lovers, if they knew how, could speak strangely
in the nocturnal air. For it seems everything conceals
us. See, the trees *abide*, the houses
40  we inhabit still stand. Only we fly
past everything like an airy exchange.
And everything conspires to keep still about us, half
as shame perhaps and half as unutterable hope.
     Lovers, you who are each fulfilled by the other,
45  you I ask about us. You clasp each other. Do you have any proof?
See, it can happen that my hands become aware
of each other or that my worn face
is protected within them. That gives me a little
sensation. But who would dare to *be* for that reason?
50  You, however, you who in each other's ecstasy
unfold until overwhelmed you entreat:
no *more*—; you who in each other's hands
grow more luxuriantly like vintage years;
you who sometimes perish because the other
55  grows too vigorously: you I ask about us. I know
you touch each other so blissfully because the caress lends endurance,
because the spot your fondness covers over does not
vanish; because underneath it you sense
pure permanence. So you almost promise yourselves eternity
60  from the embrace. And yet, when you endure
the alarm of the initial glances and the yearning by the window
and the first stroll together, *one* time through the garden:
lovers, *are* you still *in love?* When you lift your mouth
one to the other and your lips meet—: sip after sip:
65  how strangely the course of events slips from the hands of the
          partaker.

Did not the wariness of human gestures on Grecian memorial shafts
astound you? Were not love and farewell placed so gently
on their shoulders as if it were made of a different substance
than in our world? Remember the hands,
70  how lightly they repose, though the torsos are robust.

Diese Beherrschten wußten damit: so weit sind wirs,
*dieses* ist unser, uns *so* zu berühren; stärker
stemmen die Götter uns an. Doch dies ist Sache der Götter.

Fänden auch wir ein reines, verhaltenes, schmales
75  Menschliches, einen unseren Streifen Fruchtlands
zwischen Strom und Gestein. Denn das eigene Herz übersteigt uns
noch immer wie jene. Und wir können ihm nicht mehr
nachschaun in Bilder, die es besänftigen, noch in
göttliche Körper, in denen es größer sich mäßigt.

In their forbearance they knew: we have come this far,
*this* belongs to us, to touch each other *so*; the gods
put more pressure on us. But that is the choice of the gods.

75  If only we, too, could find something human that is pure,
suitable, moderate, a strip of fertile soil between
stream and rocks. For our own heart still surpasses
us just as theirs did. And we no longer can follow it
visually in pictures which assuage it nor in
divine bodies where it acquires restraint.

Eines ist, die Geliebte zu singen. Ein anderes, wehe,
jenen verborgenen schuldigen Fluß-Gott des Bluts.
Den sie von weitem erkennt, ihren Jüngling, was weiß er
selbst von dem Herren der Lust, der aus dem Einsamen oft,
5   ehe das Mädchen noch linderte, oft auch als wäre sie nicht,
ach, von welchem Unkenntlichen triefend, das Gotthaupt
aufhob, aufrufend die Nacht zu unendlichem Aufruhr.
O des Blutes Neptun, o sein furchtbarer Dreizack.
O der dunkele Wind seiner Brust aus gewundener Muschel.
10  Horch, wie die Nacht sich muldet und höhlt. Ihre Sterne,
stammt nicht von euch des Liebenden Lust zu dem Antlitz
seiner Geliebten? Hat er die innige Einsicht
in ihr reines Gesicht nicht aus dem reinen Gestirn?

Du nicht hast ihm, wehe, nicht seine Mutter
15  hat ihm die Bogen der Braun so zur Erwartung gespannt.
Nicht an dir, ihn fühlendes Mädchen, an dir nicht
bog seine Lippe sich zum fruchtbarern Ausdruck.
Meinst du wirklich, ihn hätte dein leichter Auftritt
also erschüttert, du, die wandelt wie Frühwind?
20  Zwar du erschrakst ihm das Herz; doch ältere Schrecken
stürzten in ihn bei dem berührenden Anstoß.
Ruf ihn . . . du rufst ihn nicht ganz aus dunkelem Umgang.
Freilich, er *will*, er entspringt; erleichtert gewöhnt er
sich in dein heimliches Herz und nimmt und beginnt sich.
25  Aber begann er sich je?
Mutter, *du* machtest ihn klein, du warsts, die ihn anfing;
dir war er neu, du beugtest über die neuen
Augen die freundliche Welt und wehrtest der fremden.
Wo, ach, hin sind die Jahre, da du ihm einfach
30  mit der schlanken Gestalt wallendes Chaos vertratst?
Vieles verbargst du ihm so; das nächtlich-verdächtige Zimmer
machtest du harmlos, aus deinem Herzen voll Zuflucht
mischtest du menschlichern Raum seinem Nacht-Raum hinzu.
Nicht in die Finsternis, nein, in dein näheres Dasein

# THE THIRD ELEGY

It is one thing to sing the loved one. But another, alas,
to sing the hidden culpable riverine god of the blood.
Her youthful lover whom she recognizes from afar, what does
he himself know of the lord of passion, who often,
5    before the girl's soothing, sometimes as though she did not exist,
lifted his godlike head dripping with the unknown in the lonely
youth, awakening the night to endless tumult.
O, Neptune of the blood, o, his terrible trident.
O, the dark wind of his chest from the convoluted conch.
10    Hear how the night grows hollow and cavernous. O stars,
does not the lover's delight in the face of the beloved
spring from you? Does not his fervent vision
into her pure face come from the perfect stars?

You, his mother, alas, did not tense the arch
15    of his brows into such anticipation.
Not from you, maiden who suffers him, not from you
did his lips curve into more exuberant expression.
Do you truly believe your gentle step could have agitated
him so, you who move like the morning breeze?
20    To be sure, you convulsed his heart; but older terrors
are aroused in him by the touching impulse.
Call him . . . you will not call him completely from shadowy
        company.
Certainly he *wishes* to come, he escapes; relieved he adjusts
to your secret heart and learns and begins himself.
25    But did he ever begin himself?
Mother, *you* made him small, it was you who commenced him,
to you he was new, over the new eyes you bent
the friendly world and kept the alien one away.
Where, oh, where have the years gone when you simply
30    suppressed surging chaos with your slender presence?
That way you concealed much from him; you made harmless
the room he feared at night, from the refuge of your heart
you brought more human room into his nighttime room.
You did not put his nightlight in the darkness; no, you put it

35 hast du das Nachtlicht gestellt, und es schien wie aus Freundschaft.
Nirgends ein Knistern, das du nicht lächelnd erklärtest,
so als wüßtest du längst, *wann* sich die Diele benimmt . . .
Und er horchte und linderte sich. So vieles vermochte
zärtlich dein Aufstehn; hinter den Schrank trat
40 hoch im Mantel sein Schicksal, und in die Falten des Vorhangs
paßte, die leicht sich verschob, seine unruhige Zukunft.

Und er selbst, wie er lag, der Erleichterte, unter
schläfernden Lidern deiner leichten Gestaltung
Süße lösend in den gekosteten Vorschlaf—:
45 *schien* ein Gehüteter . . . Aber *innen:* wer wehrte,
hinderte innen in ihm die Fluten der Herkunft?
Ach, da *war* keine Vorsicht im Schlafenden; schlafend,
aber träumend, aber in Fiebern: wie er sich ein-ließ.
Er, der Neue, Scheuende, wie er verstrickt war,
50 mit des innern Geschehns weiterschlagenden Ranken
schon zu Mustern verschlungen, zu würgendem Wachstum, zu
tierhaft
jagenden Formen. Wie er sich hingab—. Liebte.
Liebte sein Inneres, seines Inneren Wildnis,
diesen Urwald in ihm, auf dessen stummem Gestürztsein
55 lichtgrün sein Herz stand. Liebte. Verließ es, ging die
eigenen Wurzeln hinaus in gewaltigen Ursprung,
wo seine kleine Geburt schon überlebt war. Liebend
stieg er hinab in das ältere Blut, in die Schluchten,
wo das Furchtbare lag, noch satt von den Vätern. Und jedes
60 Schreckliche kannte ihn, blinzelte, war wie verständigt.
Ja, das Entsetzliche lächelte . . . Selten
hast du so zärtlich gelächelt, Mutter. Wie sollte
er es nicht lieben, da es ihm lächelte. *Vor* dir
hat ers geliebt, denn, da du ihn trugst schon,
65 war es im Wasser gelöst, das den Keimenden leicht macht.

Siehe, wir lieben nicht, wie die Blumen, aus einem
einzigen Jahr; uns steigt, wo wir lieben,
unvordenklicher Saft in die Arme. O Mädchen,
*dies:* daß wir liebten *in* uns, nicht Eines, ein Künftiges, sondern
70 das zahllos Brauende; nicht ein einzelnes Kind,
sondern die Väter, die wie Trümmer Gebirgs

35 in your own closer presence, and it glowed as from friendship.
Nowhere was there a rustling that you did not explain with a smile,
just as if you long had known *when* the floor creaks . . .
And he listened and was soothed. Your arising at night
was able tenderly to do much; his fate, tall in its cloak,
40 retreated behind the wardrobe, and his restive future,
easily postponed, adapted to the folds of the curtain.

And he himself, as he lay there, unburdened, under
the sleepy lids loosing the sweetness of your gentle
45 form into the drowsy foretaste of sleep—;
*seemed* protected . . . But *within,* who warded off,
who restrained the tides of inheritance within him?
Alas, in the sleeper there *was* no wariness; sleeping,
but also dreaming and feverish: how he succumbed.
He, new and easily frightened, how he was entrapped
50 by the farspreading tendrils of inner events
already entwined into patterns, into choking growth,
into animal-like chasing forms. How he surrendered—. Loved.
Loved his inner nature, the inner wilderness,
this primeval forest within, on whose silent, fallen vegetation
55 his heart stood pale green. Loved. Left it, passed along
his own roots into powerful origins
where his own little birth was already outlived. Lovingly
he descended into older blood, into the ravines
where monstrosity lay, still sated with his forefathers. And every
60 horror recognized him, winked and acted as if they agreed.
Yes, the horrors smiled . . . Rarely
have you smiled so tenderly, mother. How could he
not love them when they smiled at him? Even *before* you
he loved them, for when you were carrying him they were dispersed
65 in the fluid in which the unborn babe was suspended.

See, we do not love as the flowers do from a single year's
unfolding; when we love sap from time immemorial
rises in our arms. O maiden,
*this:* that we loved *within* us, not just one, a future one,
70 but endless fomentation; not a single maiden,
but the forefathers which rest in our depths

uns im Grunde beruhn; sondern das trockene Flußbett
einstiger Mütter—; sondern die ganze
lautlose Landschaft unter dem wolkigen oder
75   reinen Verhängnis—: *dies* kam dir, Mädchen, zuvor.

Und du selber, was weißt du—, du locktest
Vorzeit empor in dem Liebenden. Welche Gefühle
wühlten herauf aus entwandelten Wesen. Welche
Frauen haßten dich da. Was für finstere Männer
80   regtest du auf im Geäder des Jünglings? Tote
Kinder wollten zu dir . . . O leise, leise,
tu ein liebes vor ihm, ein verläßliches Tagwerk,—führ ihn
nah an den Garten heran, gieb ihm der Nächte
Übergewicht . . . . . .
                    Verhalt ihn . . . . . .

like fragments of rock, and the dried-up river bed
of earlier mothers—; the entire
soundless landscape under a cloudy or
75  clear destiny—: all *this* preceded you, oh maiden.

And you yourself, what do you know—, you tempted
bygone time up in the lover. What feelings
burrowed up from departed beings. What
women hated you then. What fierce men did
80  you arouse in the veins of the youth? Dead
children wanted to come to you . . . Oh gently, gently,
do him the service of love, a dependable labor,—lead him
near to the garden, outweigh the nights
for him . . . . . .
     Hold him . . . . . .

# DIE VIERTE ELEGIE

O Bäume Lebens, o wann winterlich?
Wir sind nicht einig. Sind nicht wie die Zug-
vögel verständigt. Überholt und spät,
so drängen wir uns plötzlich Winden auf
5    und fallen ein auf teilnahmslosen Teich.
Blühn und verdorrn ist uns zugleich bewußt.
Und irgendwo gehn Löwen noch und wissen,
solang sie herrlich sind, von keiner Ohnmacht.

Uns aber, wo wir Eines meinen, ganz,
10    ist schon des andern Aufwand fühlbar. Feindschaft
ist uns das Nächste. Treten Liebende
nicht immerfort an Ränder, eins im andern,
die sich versprachen Weite, Jagd und Heimat.
    Da wird für eines Augenblickes Zeichnung
15    ein Grund von Gegenteil bereitet, mühsam,
daß wir sie sähen; denn man ist sehr deutlich
mit uns. Wir kennen den Kontur
des Fühlens nicht: nur, was ihn formt von außen.
    Wer saß nicht bang vor seines Herzens Vorhang?
20    Der schlug sich auf: die Szenerie war Abschied.
Leicht zu verstehen. Der bekannte Garten,
und schwankte leise: dann erst kam der Tänzer.
Nicht *der.* Genug! Und wenn er auch so leicht tut,
er ist verkleidet und er wird ein Bürger
25    und geht durch seine Küche in die Wohnung.
    Ich will nicht diese halbgefüllten Masken,
lieber die Puppe. Die ist voll. Ich will
den Balg aushalten und den Draht und ihr
Gesicht aus Aussehn. Hier. Ich bin davor.
30    Wenn auch die Lampen ausgehn, wenn mir auch
gesagt wird: Nichts mehr—, wenn auch von der Bühne
das Leere herkommt mit dem grauen Luftzug,
wenn auch von meinen stillen Vorfahrn keiner
mehr mit mir dasitzt, keine Frau, sogar

# THE FOURTH ELEGY

O trees of life, o when wintry?
We are not of one mind. Unlike the migrating birds we are not
in accord. Overtaken and belated,
we suddenly wheel against the winds
5. and settle on a heedless pond.
We are simultaneously aware of flourishing and withering.
And somewhere lions still roam and are conscious of
no weakness so long as they are powerful.

We, however, when we think we know one thing with certainty
10 are already aware of the other. Animosity
is a part of us. Do not lovers who promised
themselves unlimited space, chase and sanctuary
come over and over again to verges one in the other?
    There for a momentary sketch
15 a background of contrast is readied, painstakingly,
that we might see it; for everything is made
very clear to us. We are not familiar with the contour
of emotion: only with what forms it externally.
    Is there one who has not sat anxiously before the curtain of his
      heart?
20 It raised: the scenery was farewell.
Easy to understand. The familiar garden
and it undulated gently: only then did the dancer come.
Not *that* one. Enough. Even if he acts so unsubstantial,
he is in disguise and becomes an ordinary person
25 and goes into his house through the kitchen door.
    I do not want these half-filled impersonations,
I would rather have the puppet. It is filled. I will bear patiently
with the stuffed doll and the wire and its outside
face. Here I am before it.
30 Even when the lights go out, even when
I am told: Nothing more—, even when from the stage
the emptiness blows like a gray draft,
even when of my silent forebears no one any longer
sits with me, no woman, not even

<sup>35</sup> der Knabe nicht mehr mit dem braunen Schielaug:
Ich bleibe dennoch. Es giebt immer Zuschaun.

Hab ich nicht recht? Du, der um mich so bitter
das Leben schmeckte, meines kostend, Vater,
den ersten trüben Aufguß meines Müssens,
<sup>40</sup> da ich heranwuchs, immer wieder kostend
und, mit dem Nachgeschmack so fremder Zukunft
beschäftigt, prüftest mein beschlagnes Aufschaun,—
der du, mein Vater, seit du tot bist, oft
in meiner Hoffnung, innen in mir, Angst hast,
<sup>45</sup> und Gleichmut, wie ihn Tote haben, Reiche
von Gleichmut, aufgiebst für mein bißchen Schicksal,
hab ich nicht recht? Und ihr, hab ich nicht recht,
die ihr mich liebtet für den kleinen Anfang
Liebe zu euch, von dem ich immer abkam,
<sup>50</sup> weil mir der Raum in eurem Angesicht,
da ich ihn liebte, überging in Weltraum,
in dem ihr nicht mehr wart . . . . : wenn mir zumut ist,
zu warten vor der Puppenbühne, nein,
so völlig hinzuschaun, daß, um mein Schauen
<sup>55</sup> am Ende aufzuwiegen, dort als Spieler
ein Engel hinmuß, der die Bälge hochreißt.
Engel und Puppe: dann ist endlich Schauspiel.
Dann kommt zusammen, was wir immerfort
entzwein, indem wir da sind. Dann entsteht
<sup>60</sup> aus unsern Jahreszeiten erst der Umkreis
des ganzen Wandelns. Über uns hinüber
spielt dann der Engel. Sieh, die Sterbenden,
sollten sie nicht vermuten, wie voll Vorwand
das alles ist, was wir hier leisten. Alles
<sup>65</sup> ist nicht es selbst. O Stunden in der Kindheit,
da hinter den Figuren mehr als nur
Vergangnes war und vor uns nicht die Zukunft.
Wir wuchsen freilich und wir drängten manchmal,
bald groß zu werden, denen halb zulieb,
<sup>70</sup> die andres nicht mehr hatten, als das Großsein.
Und waren doch, in unserem Alleingehn,
mit Dauerndem vergnügt und standen da

35 the boy with the immovable brown eye:
   I will stay nonetheless. One can always look on.


   Am I not right? You, father, for whom life had
   such a bitter flavor, tasting mine,
   the first murky concentrate of my necessity,
40 as I grew up tasting again and again,
   and busy with the aftertaste of such a strange
   future, you examined my sorrowful knowing glance,—
   you, my father, who often are anxious in my hope
   within me since you are dead, and sacrifice
45 your serenity, oceans of serenity such as
   the dead have, for my bit of destiny,
   am I not right? Am I not right, all of you
   who loved me for my awakening love
   for you, which always slipped away from me
50 because the space of your faces,
   when I loved it, became universal space
   and you were no longer there . . . . : when I am in a mood
   to wait before the puppet stage, no, to lose myself
   so completely that finally to respond to my
55 watching, as puppeteer an angel
   must come to animate the puppets.
   Angel and puppet: that is finally a spectacle.
   Then there comes together that which we always
   separate by our very presence. Only then does
60 there emerge from our seasons the completed cycle
   of all change. Over us then
   the angel performs. See, the dying,
   should they not sense how full of pretense
   everything is that we do here? Everything
65 is not what it seems. O hours of childhood,
   when behind the figures there was more than just
   the past and the future stood not yet before us.
   To be sure, we grew and sometimes we were in haste
   to grow up, partly for the sake of those
70 who had nothing more than being grown up.
   And yet in our loneliness we
   took pleasure in permanent things and stood there

im Zwischenraume zwischen Welt und Spielzeug,
an einer Stelle, die seit Anbeginn
75 gegründet war für einen reinen Vorgang.

Wer zeigt ein Kind, so wie es steht? Wer stellt
es ins Gestirn und giebt das Maß des Abstands
ihm in die Hand? Wer macht den Kindertod
aus grauem Brot, das hart wird,—oder läßt
80 ihn drin im runden Mund, so wie den Gröps
von einem schönen Apfel? . . . . . . Mörder sind
leicht einzusehen. Aber dies: den Tod,
den ganzen Tod, noch *vor* dem Leben so
sanft zu enthalten und nicht bös zu sein,
85 ist unbeschreiblich.

in the interval between world and toy
on a place which since the beginning of time
75 was made for a pure event.

Who portrays a child as he really is? Who places
him among the stars and puts the measuring rod
of distance in his hand? Who makes the death of a child
of gray bread that hardens,—or leaves it
80 inside in the rounded mouth like the core
of a beautiful apple? . . . . . . Murderers are
easy to understand. But this: to have death,
all of death, so gently within you,
even *before* you have lived, and yet not be angry,
85 is inexpressible.

# DIE FÜNFTE ELEGIE

*Frau Hertha Koenig zugeeignet*

Wer aber *sind* sie, sag mir, die Fahrenden, diese ein wenig
Flüchtigern noch als wir selbst, die dringend von früh an
wringt ein *wem, wem* zu Liebe
niemals zufriedener Wille? Sondern er wringt sie,
5  biegt sie, schlingt sie und schwingt sie,
wirft sie and fängt sie zurück; wie aus geölter,
glatterer Luft kommen sie nieder
auf dem verzehrten, von ihrem ewigen
Aufsprung dünneren Teppich, diesem verlorenen
10  Teppich im Weltall.
Aufgelegt wie ein Pflaster, als hätte der Vorstadt–
Himmel der Erde dort wehe getan.
                          Und kaum dort,
aufrecht, da und gezeigt: des Dastehns
großer Anfangsbuchstab . . . , schon auch, die stärksten
15  Männer, rollt sie wieder, zum Scherz, der immer
kommende Griff, wie August der Starke bei Tisch
einen zinnenen Teller.

Ach und um diese
Mitte, die Rose des Zuschauns:
20  blüht und entblättert. Um diesen
Stampfer, den Stempel, den von dem eignen
blühenden Staub getroffnen, zur Scheinfrucht
wieder der Unlust befruchteten, ihrer
niemals bewußten,—glänzend mit dünnster
25  Oberfläche leicht scheinlächelnden Unlust.

Da: der welke, faltige Stemmer,
der alte, der nur noch trommelt,
eingegangen in seiner gewaltigen Haut, als hätte sie früher
*zwei* Männer enthalten, und einer
30  läge nun schon auf dem Kirchhof, und er überlebte den andern,

# THE FIFTH ELEGY

*Dedicated to Mrs. Hertha Koenig*

Who *are* they, tell me, these homeless ones, these more fleeting
even than we ourselves, whom from the beginning on,
a never-satisfied will twists insistently for *whose*,
oh *whose* sake? Yet it twists them,
5   bends them, pitches and swings them,
throws and catches them back again; as from oiled,
smoother air they come down
on the shabby carpet worn thinner
by their continual leaps, this carpet lost
10  in the universe.
Put there like a bandage, as if the sky
of the city's edges had wounded the earth there.
                     And scarcely there,
erect, on exhibit: the large capital letter
of Defenseless endurance . . ., the next hold continually coming up
15  rolls even the strongest men, rolls them again in jest,
as King Augustus the Strong rolled up a pewter plate
at table.

Oh and around this
center the rose of onlooking:
20  blooms and sheds its petals. Around the
pounder, the pistil, fertilized by its own
prolific pollen, producing in turn
its false fruit of disdain,
of never-aware dissatisfaction,—shining with
25  slight superficial smile on the thinnest of surface.

There: the withered, wrinkled weight-lifter,
the old man, who now just beats the drum,
shrunk into his huge skin, as if it used to
contain *two* men, and one of them were already
30  in the graveyard now and he outlived the other,

taub und manchmal ein wenig
wirr, in der verwitweten Haut.

Aber der junge, der Mann, als wär er der Sohn eines Nackens
und einer Nonne: prall und strammig erfüllt
35    mit Muskeln und Einfalt.

Oh ihr,
die ein Leid, das noch klein war,
einst als Spielzeug bekam, in einer seiner
langen Genesungen . . . .

40    Du, der mit dem Aufschlag,
wie nur Früchte ihn kennen, unreif,
täglich hundertmal abfällt vom Baum der gemeinsam
erbauten Bewegung (der, rascher als Wasser, in wenig
Minuten Lenz, Sommer und Herbst hat)—
45    abfällt und anprallt ans Grab:
manchmal, in halber Pause, will dir ein liebes
Antlitz entstehn hinüber zu deiner selten
zärtlichen Mutter; doch an deinen Körper verliert sich,
der es flächig verbraucht, das schüchtern
50    kaum versuchte Gesicht . . . Und wieder
klatscht der Mann in die Hand zu dem Ansprung, und eh dir
jemals ein Schmerz deutlicher wird in der Nähe des immer
trabenden Herzens, kommt das Brennen der Fußsohln
ihm, seinem Ursprung, zuvor mit ein paar dir
55    rasch in die Augen gejagten leiblichen Tränen.
Und dennoch, blindlings,
das Lächeln . . . . .

Engel! o nimms, pflücks, das kleinblütige Heilkraut.
Schaff eine Vase, verwahrs! Stells unter jene, uns *noch* nicht
60    offenen Freuden; in lieblicher Urne
rühms mit blumiger schwungiger Aufschrift: "*Subrisio Saltat.*"

   Du dann, Liebliche,
du, von den reizendsten Freuden
stumm Übersprungne. Vielleicht sind

deaf and sometimes a little
confused in his widowed skin.

But the young one, the man, as if he were the son of a neck
and a nun: trimly and sturdily filled out
35    with muscles and innocence.

O, you,
whom a sorrow that was still small
once received as a plaything during one of its
long convalescences . . . .

40    You, who daily fall down
with a thud such as only fruits know, unripe,
a hundred times daily from the tree of conjointly
built motion (which faster than water, passes through
spring, summer and fall in a few moments)—
45    fall down and bound against the grave:
sometimes during a brief rest a loving expression
tries to form on your face for your rarely
affectionate mother; but it gets lost on your body
whose surface consumes it, the shyly,
50    scarcely tried visage . . . And again
the man claps his hands for the leap, and even
before a pain grows sharper near your constantly
pounding heart, the stinging of the footsoles
anticipates its cause with a few physical tears
55    forced quickly into your eyes.
And still, blindly,
the smile . . . . .

O, angel, take it, pick the small-flowered herb.
Get a jar and preserve it! Store it among those joys
60    *still* not revealed to us; in a graceful urn extol it
with ornately flowing inscription: "*Subrisio Saltat.*"

And then you, dear one,
you, passed over silently by the
most tempting joys. Perhaps

<sup>65</sup> deine Fransen glücklich für dich—,
oder über den jungen
prallen Brüsten die grüne metallene Seide
fühlt sich unendlich verwöhnt und entbehrt nichts.
Du,
<sup>70</sup> immerfort anders auf alle des Gleichgewichts schwankende Waagen
hingelegte Marktfrucht des Gleichmuts,
öffentlich unter den Schultern.

Wo, o *wo* ist der Ort—ich trag ihn im Herzen—,
wo sie noch lange nicht *konnten,* noch von einander
<sup>75</sup> abfieln, wie sich bespringende, nicht recht
paarige Tiere;—
wo die Gewichte noch schwer sind;
wo noch von ihren vergeblich
wirbelnden Stäben die Teller
<sup>80</sup> torkeln . . . . .

Und plötzlich in diesem mühsamen Nirgends, plötzlich
die unsägliche Stelle, wo sich das reine Zuwenig
unbegreiflich verwandelt—, umspringt
in jenes leere Zuviel.
<sup>85</sup> Wo die vielstellige Rechnung
zahlenlos aufgeht.

Plätze, o Platz in Paris, unendlicher Schauplatz,
wo die Modistin, *Madame Lamort,*
die ruhlosen Wege der Erde, endlose Bänder,
<sup>90</sup> schlingt und windet und neue aus ihnen
Schleifen erfindet, Rüschen, Blumen, Kokarden, künstliche
Früchte—, alle
unwahr gefärbt,—für die billigen
Winterhüte des Schicksals.
. . . . . . . . . . . . . . . . . . . . .

Engel!: Es wäre ein Platz, den wir nicht wissen, und dorten,
<sup>95</sup> auf unsäglichem Teppich, zeigten die Liebenden, die's hier
bis zum Können nie bringen, ihre kühnen
hohen Figuren des Herzschwungs,
ihre Türme aus Lust, ihre

65 your fringes rejoice for you—,
or over your firm young breasts
the green metallic silk feels
infinitely indulged and in want of nothing.
You,
70 proffered in continual variations on all the swaying scales
of equilibrium, fruit of equanimity for sale
in the public marketplace in the midst of the shoulders.

Where, oh *where* is the place—I carry it in my heart—,
where they were still far from *perfection*, still
75 fell apart like improperly paired animals
in mating;—
where the weights still are heavy;
where the plates still fly off
their vainly twirling
80 staves . . . . .

And suddenly in this laborious nowhere, suddenly
the indescribable spot, where mere insufficiency
incomprehensibly changes—, is transformed
into empty perfection.
85 Where the complex equation
balances.

Plazas, o plaza in Paris, infinite show place,
where the milliner, *Madame Lamort*,
weaves and winds the restless roads of the earth,
90 endless ribbons, and designs new bows
from them, frills, flowers, cockades, artificial fruits—,
all unnaturally colored,—for the cheap
winter hats of destiny.
. . . . . . . . . . . . . . . . . . . .

Angel!: There may be a place which we do not know, and there
95 on an indescribable carpet lovers, who could not reach
perfection here, would display their bold
sublime feats of the soaring heart,
their spires of rapture, their ladders,

längst, wo Boden nie war, nur an einander
100    lehnenden Leitern, bebend,—und *könntens*,
         vor den Zuschauern rings, unzähligen lautlosen Toten:
                Würfen die dann ihre letzten, immer ersparten,
         immer verborgenen, die wir nicht kennen, ewig
         gültigen Münzen des Glücks vor das endlich
105    wahrhaft lächelnde Paar auf gestilltem
         Teppich?

where there never has been ground, long leaning
100  against each other alone, trembling,—and they would *succeed*,
before the surrounding spectators, the innumerable silent dead:
     Would these then throw their last saved-up
hidden-away eternally valid coins
of good fortune, which are unknown to us,
105  before the couple truly smiling at last on the
stilled carpet?

# DIE SECHSTE ELEGIE

Feigenbaum, seit wie lange schon ists mir bedeutend,
wie du die Blüte beinah ganz überschlägst
und hinein in die zeitig entschlossene Frucht,
ungerühmt, drängst dein reines Geheimnis.
5  Wie der Fontäne Rohr treibt dein gebognes Gezweig
abwärts den Saft und hinan: und er springt aus dem Schlaf,
fast nicht erwachend, ins Glück seiner süßesten Leistung.
Sieh: wie der Gott in den Schwan.
      . . . . . . Wir aber verweilen,
ach, uns rühmt es zu blühn, und ins verspätete Innre
10  unserer endlichen Frucht gehn wir verraten hinein.
Wenigen steigt so stark der Andrang des Handelns,
daß sie schon anstehn und glühn in der Fülle des Herzens,
wenn die Verführung zum Blühn wie gelinderte Nachtluft
ihnen die Jugend des Munds, ihnen die Lider berührt:
15  Helden vielleicht und den frühe Hinüberbestimmten,
denen der gärtnernde Tod anders die Adern verbiegt.
Diese stürzen dahin: dem eigenen Lächeln
sind sie voran, wie das Rossegespann in den milden
muldigen Bildern von Karnak dem siegenden König.

20  Wunderlich nah ist der Held doch den jugendlich Toten. Dauern
ficht ihn nicht an. Sein Aufgang ist Dasein; beständig
nimmt er sich fort und tritt ins veränderte Sternbild
seiner steten Gefahr. Dort fänden ihn wenige. Aber,
das uns finster verschweigt, das plötzlich begeisterte Schicksal
25  singt ihn hinein in den Sturm seiner aufrauschenden Welt.
Hör ich doch keinen wie *ihn*. Auf einmal durchgeht mich
mit der strömenden Luft sein verdunkelter Ton.

Dann, wie verbärg ich mich gern vor der Sehnsucht: O wär ich,
wär ich ein Knabe und dürft es noch werden und säße
30  in die künftigen Arme gestützt und läse von Simson,
wie seine Mutter erst nichts und dann alles gebar.

# THE SIXTH ELEGY

Fig tree, how long it has impressed me,
that you almost pass over blossoming,
and into the promptly revealed fruit,
unglorified, pack your unbroken secret.
5   Like the pipe of the fountain your arched branches
drive the sap downward and up again: and almost without
         awakening
it leaps from sleep, into the joy of its sweetest achievement.
See: like the god in the swan.
                        . . . . . . We however tarry,
alas, we boast of blossoming and deluded we proceed
10  into the belated interior of our finite final fruit.
In only a few is the urge for action so strong
that they already stand prepared and glow in their heart's abundance
when the enticement to bloom touches the youth of their mouths
and their eyelids like the mild nocturnal air:
15  heroes perhaps and those destined to die young,
in whom the husbandman Death bends the veins differently.
These rush on: they precede their own smile
like the span of horses before the victorious king
in the weathered and worn images in Karnak.

20  Yes, the hero is strangely akin to those who die young. He is
not concerned with enduring. His very ascent is permanence;
he is forever moving onward into the changed constellation
of his continual danger where only a few could find him.
But suddenly enraptured fate, which about us is so darkly silent,
25  exalts him into the storm of his onrushing world.
I hear none other like *him*. Suddenly his muffled voice
passes through me, borne by the flowing air.

How gladly I would hide then from the yearning: oh, if I
were only a boy again and could make my life anew
30  and were sitting leaning on arms yet to be and reading of Samson,
how his mother bore nothing at first and then everything.

35

War er nicht Held schon in dir, o Mutter, begann nicht
dort schon, in dir, seine herrische Auswahl?
Tausende brauten im Schooß und wollten *er* sein,
35  aber sieh: er ergriff und ließ aus—, wählte und konnte.
Und wenn er Säulen zerstieß, so wars, da er ausbrach
aus der Welt deines Leibs in die engere Welt, wo er weiter
wählte und konnte. O Mütter der Helden, o Ursprung
reißender Ströme! Ihr Schluchten, in die sich
40  hoch von dem Herzrand, klagend,
schon die Mädchen gestürzt, künftig die Opfer dem Sohn.
    Denn hinstürmte der Held durch Aufenthalte der Liebe,
jeder hob ihn hinaus, jeder ihn meinende Herzschlag,
abgewendet schon, stand er am Ende der Lächeln,—anders.

Was he not a hero even within you, o mother, did not his
imperious choice begin there within you?
35  Thousands were stirring in the womb, wanting to be *him*,
but see: he took hold and cast them out—, chose and prevailed.
And if ever he brought down pillars, it was when he burst forth
from the world of your body into the narrower world, where he
continued to choose and prevail. O, mothers of heroes,
40  o source of rampaging streams! Ravines into which
maidens have already plunged in sorrow
from the high rim of the heart, future victims of the son.

For when the hero dashed through intervals of love,
each beat of the heart meant for him only lifted him beyond it;
already estranged, when the smiles were past he was different.

# DIE SIEBENTE ELEGIE

Werbung nicht mehr, nicht Werbung, entwachsene Stimme,
sei deines Schreies Natur; zwar schrieest du rein wie der Vogel,
wenn ihn die Jahreszeit aufhebt, die steigende, beinah vergessend,
daß er ein kümmerndes Tier und nicht nur ein einzelnes Herz sei,
5   das sie ins Heitere wirft, in die innigen Himmel. Wie er, so
würbest du wohl, nicht minder—, daß, noch unsichtbar,
dich die Freundin erführ, die stille, in der eine Antwort
langsam erwacht und über dem Hören sich anwärmt,—
deinem erkühnten Gefühl die erglühte Gefühlin.

10   O und der Frühling begriffe—, da ist keine Stelle,
die nicht trüge den Ton der Verkündigung. Erst jenen kleinen
fragenden Auflaut, den, mit steigernder Stille,
weithin umschweigt ein reiner bejahender Tag.
Dann die Stufen hinan, Ruf-Stufen hinan, zum geträumten
15   Tempel der Zukunft—; dann den Triller, Fontäne,
die zu dem drängenden Strahl schon das Fallen zuvornimmt
im versprechlichen Spiel . . . . Und vor sich, den Sommer.
     Nicht nur die Morgen alle des Sommers—, nicht nur
wie sie sich wandeln in Tag und strahlen vor Anfang.
20   Nicht nur die Tage, die zart sind um Blumen, und oben,
um die gestalteten Bäume, stark und gewaltig.
Nicht nur die Andacht dieser entfalteten Kräfte,
nicht nur die Wege, nicht nur die Wiesen im Abend,
nicht nur, nach spätem Gewitter, das atmende Klarsein,
25   nicht nur der nahende Schlaf und ein Ahnen, abends . . .
sondern die Nächte! Sondern die hohen, des Sommers,
Nächte, sondern die Sterne, die Sterne der Erde.
O einst tot sein und sie wissen unendlich,
alle die Sterne: denn wie, wie, wie sie vergessen!

30   Siehe, da rief ich die Liebende. Aber nicht *sie* nur
käme . . . Es kämen aus schwächlichen Gräbern
Mädchen und ständen . . . Denn, wie beschränk ich,
wie, den gerufenen Ruf? Die Versunkenen suchen

# THE SEVENTH ELEGY

May wooing no more, not wooing, be the nature of your cry,
outgrown voice; though you could call as ethereally as the bird
when the season propels it upward, almost forgetting
that it is a poor living creature and not heart alone,
5  which is thrust into the light, into the intense sky. Like it
you would woo no less perfectly—, so that, still unseen,
she would sense your presence, the silent friend, in whom
an answer slowly awakens and grows warmer with perception,—
the ardent companion to your own emboldened feeling.

10  Oh, and springtime would understand—, nowhere is there a place
which would not convey the announcement. In the beginning
the sound of a tiny question, which a perfect day in approval
encloses all around with ever increasing silence.
Then up the stairway, up the staircase of sound, to the envisioned
15  temple of the future—; then the trill, fountain
whose rising jet anticipates already its fall
in predictable play . . . . And still ahead, the summer.
    Not only all the dawns of summer—, not only
how they change into day and radiate with beginning.
20  Not only the days which are gentle near flowers and strong
and powerful near the tops of fully formed trees.
Not only the reverence of these unfolded powers,
not only the roads, not only the meadows in the evening,
not only the refreshing clearness after a late thunderstorm,
25  not only approaching sleep and a premonition, in the evening . . .
but the nights! The vast nights of summer
and the stars, the stars of our earth.
Oh, to be dead some day and know them perfectly,
all the stars: for how, how, how can we forget them!

30  See, I could call the beloved. But *she* would not come
alone . . . From insecure graves maidens would come and
stand there . . . For how, oh how, could I restrict
my summons? The deprived still

immer noch Erde.— Ihr Kinder, ein hiesig
35   einmal ergriffenes Ding gälte für viele.
Glaubt nicht, Schicksal sei mehr, als das Dichte der Kindheit;
wie überholtet ihr oft den Geliebten, atmend,
atmend nach seligem Lauf, auf nichts zu, ins Freie.

Hiersein ist herrlich. Ihr wußtet es, Mädchen, *ihr* auch,
40   die ihr scheinbar entbehrtet, versankt—, ihr, in den ärgsten
Gassen der Städte, Schwärende, oder dem Abfall
Offene. Denn eine Stunde war jeder, vielleicht nicht
ganz eine Stunde, ein mit den Maßen der Zeit kaum
Meßliches zwischen zwei Weilen—, da sie ein Dasein
45   hatte. Alles. Die Adern voll Dasein.
Nur, wir vergessen so leicht, was der lachende Nachbar
uns nicht bestätigt oder beneidet. Sichtbar
wollen wirs heben, wo doch das sichtbarste Glück uns
erst zu erkennen sich giebt, wenn wir es innen verwandeln.

50   Nirgends, Geliebte, wird Welt sein, als innen. Unser
Leben geht hin mit Verwandlung. Und immer geringer
schwindet das Außen. Wo einmal ein dauerndes Haus war,
schlägt sich erdachtes Gebild vor, quer, zu Erdenklichem
völlig gehörig, als ständ es noch ganz im Gehirne.
55   Weite Speicher der Kraft schafft sich der Zeitgeist, gestaltlos
wie der spannende Drang, den er aus allem gewinnt.
Tempel kennt er nicht mehr. Diese, des Herzens, Verschwendung
sparen wir heimlicher ein. Ja, wo noch eins übersteht,
ein einst gebetetes Ding, ein gedientes, geknietes—,
60   hält es sich, so wie es ist, schon ins Unsichtbare hin.
Viele gewahrens nicht mehr, doch ohne den Vorteil,
daß sie's nun *innerlich* baun, mit Pfeilern und Statuen, größer!
    Jede dumpfe Umkehr der Welt hat solche Enterbte,
denen das Frühere nicht und noch nicht das Nächste gehört.
65   Denn auch das Nächste ist weit für die Menschen. *Uns* soll
dies nicht verwirren; es stärke in uns die Bewahrung
der noch erkannten Gestalt.— Dies *stand* einmal unter Menschen,
mitten im Schicksal stands, im vernichtenden, mitten
im Nichtwissen-Wohin stand es, wie seiend, und bog
70   Sterne zu sich aus gesicherten Himmeln. Engel,

40

seek the earth. —Children, a single thing once truly
35  understood here would take the place of many.
Do not think that destiny is more than the intensity of childhood;
how often you overtook the beloved, out of breath,
panting after blissful chase, passed on into openness.

Earthly existence is wonderful. *You* knew it, too, you maidens,
40  you who seemed deprived and vanished—, you in the worst
parts of the cities, festering, or open
to destruction. For each one had an hour, perhaps
not quite an hour, a time between two spans scarcely
measureable with the measures of time—, when she
45  truly lived. Had everything. Veins filled with life.
But we forget so easily what our laughing neighbor
does not confirm or envy. We want
to hold it up visibly, though the most obvious good fortune
cannot be comprehended until we transform it within us.

50  Nowhere, beloved, will be life but within us. Our
life passes by in change. And the outer world
shrinks into less and less. Where once was an enduring house,
a cerebral structure arises, obliquely, an entirely
rational product, as if it still stood in the mind.
55  Our age constructs for itself huge storehouses of power, amorphous
as the tense energy which it wins from everything.—
No longer is it familiar with temples. These, extravagance of the
     heart,
we save up more secretively. Where one of them still survives,
a once venerated thing, served and worshiped—
60  it reaches already, just as it is, into the invisible world.
Many no longer perceive it, but without the advantage
of building it now *within*, with pillars and statues—, greater!
     Each sluggish change in the world has such dispossessed ones
to whom what has been belongs not nor yet what is to come.
65  For even what is close to man is still far. This should
not confuse *us;* let it strengthen us in preservation
of the still discernable form.—Once this *stood* among men,
in the midst of destiny, of destructive fortune, in the midst
of not-knowing-whither it stood as if enduring and drew
70  down stars from the securely established heavens. Angel,

*dir* noch zeig ich es, *da!* in deinem Anschaun
steh es gerettet zuletzt, nun endlich aufrecht.
Säulen, Pylone, der Sphinx, das strebende Stemmen,
grau aus vergehender Stadt oder aus fremder, des Doms.

75 War es nicht Wunder? O staune, Engel, denn *wir* sinds,
wir, o du Großer, erzähls, daß wir solches vermochten, mein Atem
reicht für die Rühmung nicht aus. So haben wir dennoch
nicht die Räume versäumt, diese gewährenden, diese
*unseren* Räume. (Was müssen sie fürchterlich groß sein,
80 da sie Jahrtausende nicht unseres Fühlns überfülln.)
Aber ein Turm war groß, nicht wahr? O Engel, er war es,—
groß, auch noch neben dir? Chartres war groß—, und Musik
reichte noch weiter hinan und überstieg uns. Doch selbst nur
eine Liebende—, oh, allein am nächtlichen Fenster . . . .
85 reichte sie dir nicht ans Knie—?
                                    Glaub *nicht*, daß ich werbe.
Engel, und würb ich dich auch! Du kommst nicht. Denn mein
Anruf ist immer voll Hinweg; wider so starke
Strömung kannst du nicht schreiten. Wie ein gestreckter
Arm ist mein Rufen. Und seine zum Greifen
90 oben offene Hand bleibt vor dir
offen, wie Abwehr und Warnung,
Unfaßlicher, weitauf.

I will show it still existing to *you, there!* In your contemplation
may it stand rescued at last, finally upright.
Pillars, pylons, the Sphinx, the soaring thrust
of a cathedral, gray, in decaying towns or in strange ones.

75    Was it not a miracle? Marvel, o Angel, for it is *we,*
we, o great one; proclaim that we were capable of such, my breath
is not ample for such praise. So we have not neglected
these spaces after all, these enduring spaces,
*our* spaces. (How terribly large they must be,
80    when milleniums of our experience have not overcrowded them.)
But a spire was great, was it not? O, Angel, it was,—
great even beside you? Chartres was great—, and music
reached up still farther and transcended us. Yet even
just a girl in love—, alone by the window at night . . . .
85    did she not reach up to your knee—?

                          Do *not* believe that I plead.
Angel, even though I should summon you, you will not come. For
my summons is ever full of renunciation; you cannot come
against so strong a current. My call is like
an outstretched arm. And the hand
90    at the end is open, stays open
before you, incomprehensible being,
spread out, as defense and forewarning.

# DIE ACHTE ELEGIE

*Rudolf Kassner zugeeignet*

Mit allen Augen sieht die Kreatur
das Offene. Nur unsre Augen sind
wie umgekehrt und ganz um sie gestellt
als Fallen, rings um ihren freien Ausgang.
5   Was draußen *ist*, wir wissens aus des Tiers
Antlitz allein; denn schon das frühe Kind
wenden wir um und zwingens, daß es rückwärts
Gestaltung sehe, nicht das Offne, das
im Tiergesicht so tief ist. Frei von Tod.
10   *Ihn* sehen wir allein; das freie Tier
hat seinen Untergang stets hinter sich
und vor sich Gott, und wenn es geht, so gehts
in Ewigkeit, so wie die Brunnen gehen.
    *Wir* haben nie, nicht einen einzigen Tag,
15   den reinen Raum vor uns, in den die Blumen
unendlich aufgehn. Immer ist es Welt
und niemals Nirgends ohne Nicht: das Reine,
Unüberwachte, das man atmet und
unendlich *weiß* und nicht begehrt. Als Kind
20   verliert sich eins im Stilln an dies und wird
gerüttelt. Oder jener stirbt und *ists*.
Denn nah am Tod sieht man den Tod nicht mehr
und starrt *hinaus*, vielleicht mit großem Tierblick.
Liebende, wäre nicht der andre, der
25   die Sicht verstellt, sind nah daran und staunen . . .
Wie aus Versehn ist ihnen aufgetan
hinter dem andern . . . Aber über ihn
kommt keiner fort, und wieder wird ihm Welt.
Der Schöpfung immer zugewendet, sehn
30   wir nur auf ihr die Spiegelung des Frein,
von uns verdunkelt. Oder daß ein Tier,
ein stummes, aufschaut, ruhig durch uns durch.
Dieses heißt Schicksal: gegenüber sein
und nichts als das und immer gegenüber.

# THE EIGHTH ELEGY

*Dedicated to Rudolf Kassner*

With all its eyes the animal sees
openness. Our eyes alone are as if
reversed and set all around it
like traps, surrounding its unhindered departure.
5  What *exists* beyond, we know only from the countenance
of the animal; for we turn even
the child around and force it to look back
at creation, not at the openness embedded
so deeply in the animal face. Free from death.
10  Only we see *death;* the free animal
always has death behind it
and before it God, and when it moves, it moves
in eternity just as the fountains do.
*We* never have ahead of us, not for a single day,
15  the pure space into which the flowers
forever unfold. It is always our human world
and never a nowhere without the negative: that which is
pure and unconstrained, which one breathes in
and *knows* perfectly and does not desire. As a child
20  one gets lost there in the quiet and is recalled
by a shake. Or someone dies and *is* it.
For when death approaches one no longer sees death,
but gazes *beyond*, perhaps with the great look of the animal.
Lovers, if it were not for the other, who
25  obstructs the view, are near to it and marvel . . .
As by error it opens for them
beyond the beloved . . . But neither can
move past the other, and again the world crowds in.
Always turned toward our concrete world, we see
30  in it only the reflection of boundlessness
dimmed by ourselves. Or an animal,
a dumb animal, looks up and calmly through us.
This is called destiny: always to be on the outside,
nothing but that, and always shut out.

45

<sup>35</sup> Wäre Bewußtheit unsrer Art in dem
sicheren Tier, das uns entgegenzieht
in anderer Richtung—, riß es uns herum
mit seinem Wandel. Doch sein Sein ist ihm
unendlich, ungefaßt und ohne Blick
<sup>40</sup> auf seinen Zustand, rein, so wie sein Ausblick.
Und wo wir Zukunft sehn, dort sieht es Alles
und sich in Allem und geheilt für immer.

Und doch ist in dem wachsam warmen Tier
Gewicht und Sorge einer großen Schwermut.
<sup>45</sup> Denn ihm auch haftet immer an, was uns
oft überwältigt,—die Erinnerung,
als sei schon einmal das, wonach man drängt,
näher gewesen, treuer und sein Anschluß
unendlich zärtlich. Hier ist alles Abstand,
<sup>50</sup> und dort wars Atem. Nach der ersten Heimat
ist ihm die zweite zwitterig und windig.
     O Seligkeit der *kleinen* Kreatur,
die immer *bleibt* im Schooße, der sie austrug;
o Glück der Mücke, die noch *innen* hüpft,
<sup>55</sup> selbst wenn sie Hochzeit hat: denn Schooß ist Alles.
Und sieh die halbe Sicherheit des Vogels,
der beinah beides weiß aus seinem Ursprung,
als wär er eine Seele der Etrusker,
aus einem Toten, den ein Raum empfing,
<sup>60</sup> doch mit der ruhenden Figur als Deckel.
Und wie bestürzt ist eins, das fliegen muß
und stammt aus einem Schooß. Wie vor sich selbst
erschreckt, durchzuckts die Luft, wie wenn ein Sprung
durch eine Tasse geht. So reißt die Spur
<sup>65</sup> der Fledermaus durchs Porzellan des Abends.

Und wir: Zuschauer, immer, überall,
dem allen zugewandt und nie hinaus!
Uns überfüllts. Wir ordnens. Es zerfällt.
Wir ordnens wieder und zerfallen selbst.

<sup>70</sup> Wer hat uns also umgedreht, daß wir,
was wir auch tun, in jener Haltung sind

35 If awareness such as ours existed in the
confident animal that approaches us
moving in a different direction—, it would pull us around
with its passing. But for it Being is
boundless, unlimited, without regard
40 for its condition, as pure as its own sure gaze.
And where we look at the future, there it beholds totality
and itself within totality and forever whole.

Yet within the attentively warm blooded animal is
the weight and care of a great sadness.
45 For there always clings to it that which
often overpowers us,—a memory,
as if that which man pursues had already
been closer once, more secure, and union with it
infinitely tender. Here everything is separation, while there
50 it was like breathing. After the first home
its second is ambiguous and drafty.
    Oh the blessedness of the *tiny* creature,
which forever *stays* in the womb that bore it;
oh, the happiness of the insect that still hops *within*,
55 even when it weds: for all is womb.
And see the half-assurance of the bird,
which from its origin is almost aware of both worlds,
as if it were an Etruscan soul
from a dead man in the space which received him,
60 but with the reclining figure as cover.
And how perplexed is the creature that must fly
and yet comes from a womb. As if afraid of
itself, it flashes through the air like a crack
appearing in a cup. So the tracery of the bat
65 flashes through the porcelain of the evening.

And we: spectators, everywhere, all the time,
turned toward the world of things and never beyond!
It fills us. We arrange it. It perishes.
We arrange it again and perish ourselves.

70 Who has thus turned us around, that
whatever we may do, we are always in the posture

von einem, welcher fortgeht? Wie er auf
dem letzten Hügel, der ihm ganz sein Tal
noch einmal zeigt, sich wendet, anhält, weilt—,
75   so leben wir und nehmen immer Abschied.

of one who is departing? As on the last elevation
which spreads before him once more
all his valley, he turns around, stops and lingers—,
75   thus do we live, forever taking leave.

# DIE NEUNTE ELEGIE

Warum, wenn es angeht, also die Frist des Daseins
hinzubringen, als Lorbeer, ein wenig dunkler als alles
andere Grün, mit kleinen Wellen an jedem
Blattrand (wie eines Windes Lächeln)—: warum dann
5   Menschliches müssen—und, Schicksal vermeidend,
sich sehnen nach Schicksal? . . .

               Oh, *nicht* weil Glück *ist,*
dieser voreilige Vorteil eines nahen Verlusts.
Nicht aus Neugier, oder zur Übung des Herzens,
das auch im Lorbeer *wäre* . . . . .

10   Aber weil Hiersein viel ist, und weil uns scheinbar
alles das Hiesige braucht, dieses Schwindende, das
seltsam uns angeht. Uns, die Schwindendsten. *Ein* Mal
jedes, nur *ein* Mal. *Ein* Mal und nichtmehr. Und wir auch
*ein* Mal. Nie wieder. Aber dieses
15   *ein* Mal gewesen zu sein, wenn auch nur *ein* Mal:
*irdisch* gewesen zu sein, scheint nicht widerrufbar.

Und so drängen wir uns und wollen es leisten,
wollens enthalten in unsern einfachen Händen,
im überfüllteren Blick und im sprachlosen Herzen.
20   Wollen es werden.—Wem es geben? Am liebsten
alles behalten für immer . . . Ach, in den andern Bezug
wehe, was nimmt man hinüber? Nicht das Anschaun, das hier
langsam erlernte, und kein hier Ereignetes. Keins.
Also die Schmerzen. Also vor allem das Schwersein,
25   also der Liebe lange Erfahrung,— also
lauter Unsägliches. Aber später,
unter den Sternen, was solls: *die* sind *besser* unsäglich.
Bringt doch der Wanderer auch vom Hange des Bergrands
nicht eine Hand voll Erde ins Tal, die Allen unsägliche, sondern
30   ein erworbenes Wort, reines, den gelben und blaun
Enzian. Sind wir vielleicht *hier,* um zu sagen: Haus,

# THE NINTH ELEGY

Why if it is possible to pass the
span of life as laurel, a little darker than all the
other green with little waves around the edge
of the leaf (like the smile of a breeze)—: why then
5   the necessity to be human—and evading destiny,
yet to yearn for destiny? . . .

                        Oh *not* because happiness *exists*,
this fleeting benefit of impending destruction.
Not because of curiosity nor as training for the heart,
which likewise *would exist* in the laurel . . . . .

10   But because earthly existence means much, and because apparently
everything here needs us, this fleeting reality which
strangely concerns us. Us, the most fleeting of all. Just
*once*, everything, just *one* time. *One* time and no more. And we, too,
*once*. Never again. But to have existed
15   this *once*, even if only *one* time:
to have existed *here on earth*, appears irrevocable.

And so we press on and try to accomplish it,
try to hold it in our simple hands,
in our fuller glance and in our speechless heart.
20   Try to become it.—To give it to whom? Best of all
to hold on to it all forever . . . Alas, to the other realm,
oh, what can we take along? Not our contemplation so
slowly learned here and nothing that has happened here. Nothing.
The suffering then. Above all the burden of life,
25   the long experience of love—, only
inexpressible things. But later,
among the stars, what is the use: *they* are more inexpressible still.
For from the rugged mountain slope the traveler does not bring
      back
a handful of earth to the valley, inexpressible to everyone, but
30   an acquired word, a perfect one, the blue and yellow
gentian. Perhaps we are *here* to say: house,

Brücke, Brunnen, Tor, Krug, Obstbaum, Fenster,—
höchstens: Säule, Turm . . . . aber zu *sagen*, verstehs,
oh zu sagen *so*, wie selber die Dinge niemals
35 innig meinten zu sein. Ist nicht die heimliche List
dieser verschwiegenen Erde, wenn sie die Liebenden drängt,
daß sich in ihrem Gefühl jedes und jedes entzückt?
Schwelle: was ists für zwei
Liebende, daß sie die eigne ältere Schwelle der Tür
40 ein wenig verbrauchen, auch sie, nach den vielen vorher
und vor den Künftigen . . . ., leicht.

*Hier* ist des *Säglichen* Zeit, *hier* seine Heimat.
Sprich und bekenn. Mehr als je
fallen die Dinge dahin, die erlebbaren, denn,
45 was sie verdrängend ersetzt, ist ein Tun ohne Bild.
Tun unter Krusten, die willig zerspringen, sobald
innen das Handeln entwächst und sich anders begrenzt.
Zwischen den Hämmern besteht
unser Herz, wie die Zunge
50 zwischen den Zähnen, die doch,
dennoch, die preisende bleibt.

Preise dem Engel die Welt, nicht die unsägliche, *ihm*
kannst du nicht großtun mit herrlich Erfühltem; im Weltall,
wo er fühlender fühlt, bist du ein Neuling. Drum zeig
55 ihm das Einfache, das, von Geschlecht zu Geschlechtern gestaltet,
als ein Unsriges lebt, neben der Hand und im Blick.
Sag ihm die Dinge. Er wird staunender stehn; wie du standest
bei dem Seiler in Rom, oder beim Töpfer am Nil.
Zeig ihm, wie glücklich ein Ding sein kann, wie schuldlos und
unser,
60 wie selbst das klagende Leid rein zur Gestalt sich entschließt,
dient als ein Ding, oder stirbt in ein Ding—, und jenseits
selig der Geige entgeht. —Und diese, von Hingang
lebenden Dinge verstehn, daß du sie rühmst; vergänglich,
traun sie ein Rettendes uns, den Vergänglichsten, zu.
65 Wollen, wir sollen sie ganz im unsichtbarn Herzen verwandeln
in—o unendlich—in uns! Wer wir am Ende auch seien.

Erde, ist es nicht dies, was du willst: *unsichtbar*

bridge, fountain, gateway, jug, fruit tree, window—,
at the most: pillar, spire . . . . but to *say* them, you understand,
oh to say them in *such* a way, as even the things themselves never
35   dared to imagine to be. Is it not the hidden craft
of this taciturn earth, when it urges the lovers,
that in their emotion the whole world is enraptured?
Threshold: how easy it is for two
lovers that they add a little more wear to the already worn sill
40   of their door, they too, after the many before them
and before those yet to come.

*Here* is the time of the *expressible, here* is its home.
Speak out and acknowledge it. More than ever before
the things which can be experienced are vanishing, for
45   what is crowding out and replacing them is act without image.
Action under a shell which easily breaks apart as soon as
the business within enlarges and takes on new shape.
Between the hammers our heart
endures, like the tongue
50   between the teeth, which yet
continues to praise.

Praise the world to the angel, not the inexpressible one, you
cannot impress *him* with splendid emotion; in the cosmos
where he feels more feelingly, you are but a newcomer. So show
55   him what is simple, made by generation after generation,
which lives in our hand and our sight as our own.
Tell him the things. He will stand more astonished; as you
stood by the rope-maker in Rome or the potter by the Nile.
Show him how happy a thing can be, how innocent and part of us,
60   how even mournful sorrow chastely chooses to take on form,
serves as a thing or dies in a thing—, and blissfully
sings beyond the violin. —And these things which
live by perishing understand that you praise them; passing away,
they look to us for rescue, to us the most fleeting of all.
65   They desire for us to transform them in our invisible hearts
within—oh infinitely—within us! Whatever we may ultimately be.

Earth, is this not what you want: to arise within us

in uns erstehn?— Ist es dein Traum nicht,
einmal unsichtbar zu sein?—Erde! unsichtbar!
70 Was, wenn Verwandlung nicht, ist dein drängender Auftrag?
Erde, du liebe, ich will. Oh glaub, es bedürfte
nicht deiner Frühlinge mehr, mich dir zu gewinnen—, *einer*
ach, ein einziger ist schon dem Blute zu viel.
Namenlos bin ich zu dir entschlossen, von weit her.
75 Immer warst du im Recht, und dein heiliger Einfall
ist der vertrauliche Tod.

Siehe, ich lebe. Woraus? Weder Kindheit noch Zukunft
werden weniger . . . . . Überzähliges Dasein
entspringt mir im Herzen.

*invisibly?*— Is it not your dream
some day to be invisible?—Earth: invisible!
70   What if not transformation is your urgent commission?
Earth, oh good earth, I will. Oh, do not believe that
more of your springtimes are needed to win me—, *one*
oh, a single one, is already too much for my blood.
Namelessly I have belonged to you from the beginning.
75   You have always been right and familiar death
is your blessed inspiration.

See, I live. From what? Neither childhood nor future
grow less . . . . . Abundant life
leaps up in my heart.

# DIE ZEHNTE ELEGIE

Daß ich dereinst, an dem Ausgang der grimmigen Einsicht,
Jubel und Ruhm aufsinge zustimmenden Engeln.
Daß von den klar geschlagenen Hämmern des Herzens
keiner versage an weichen, zweifelnden oder
5   reißenden Saiten. Daß mich mein strömendes Antlitz
glänzender mache; daß das unscheinbare Weinen
blühe. O wie werdet ihr dann, Nächte, mir lieb sein,
gehärmte. Daß ich euch knieender nicht, untröstliche Schwestern,
hinnahm, nicht in euer gelöstes
10  Haar mich gelöster ergab. Wir, Vergeuder der Schmerzen.
Wie wir sie absehn voraus, in die traurige Dauer,
ob sie nicht enden vielleicht. Sie aber sind ja
unser winterwähriges Laub, unser dunkeles Sinngrün,
*eine* der Zeiten des heimlichen Jahres—, nicht nur
15  Zeit—, sind Stelle, Siedelung, Lager, Boden, Wohnort.

Freilich, wehe, wie fremd sind die Gassen der Leidstadt,
wo in der falschen, aus Übertönung gemachten
Stille, stark, aus der Gußform des Leeren der Ausguß
prahlt: der vergoldete Lärm, das platzende Denkmal.
20  O, wie spurlos zerträte ein Engel ihnen den Trostmarkt,
den die Kirche begrenzt, ihre fertig gekaufte:
reinlich und zu und enttäuscht wie ein Postamt am Sonntag.
Draußen aber kräuseln sich immer die Ränder von Jahrmarkt.
Schaukeln der Freiheit! Taucher und Gaukler des Eifers!
25  Und des behübschten Glücks figürliche Schießstatt,
wo es zappelt von Ziel und sich blechern benimmt,
wenn ein Geschickterer trifft. Von Beifall zu Zufall
taumelt er weiter; denn Buden jeglicher Neugier
werben, trommeln und plärrn. Für Erwachsene aber
30  ist noch besonders zu sehn, wie das Geld sich vermehrt, anatomisch,
nicht zur Belustigung nur: der Geschlechtsteil des Gelds,
alles, das Ganze, der Vorgang—, das unterrichtet und macht
fruchtbar . . . . . . . .
. . . . Oh aber gleich darüber hinaus,

# THE TENTH ELEGY

Someday, at the end of this grim perception,
may I sing joy and praise to approving angels.
May none of the clearly struck hammers of the heart
fail by striking slack, wavering or
5    breaking strings. May the tears which stream from my countenance
make me more radiant; may unpretentious weeping
flourish. Oh how I will cherish you then, nights filled with
sorrow. Inconsolable sisters, why did I not kneel more submissively
to accept you, why did I not surrender with greater abandon
10    to your loosened hair? We, squanderers of sorrows.
In the way we calculate them in advance, looking askance at their
mournful duration, and wondering if they might not end. Yet they
       are
our permanent winter foliage, our dark evergreen of meaning,
*one* of the seasons of our secret year—, not only
15    season—, they are place, outpost, camp, soil, dwelling place.

Alas, how strange indeed are the streets of the City of Grief,
where in the unreal silence made of drowned-out
noise the figure cast from the hollow form of emptiness
boasts loudly: the gilded noise, the ostentatious memorial.
20    How completely an angel would crush their market of consolation
which the church adjoins, bought ready-made:
cleaned up and closed and frustrated like a post office on Sunday.
Outside, however, the edges continually curl with carnival.
Swings of freedom! Divers and jugglers of eagerness!
25    And the figurative shooting gallery of prettied-up good fortune,
where the targets gyrate and clang tinnily
when a more skillful shot hits one. From cheers to chance
he reels on; for booths with all sorts of attractions
entice and drum and shout. For adults only, however,
30    to one side there is to be seen how money multiplies, anatomically,
not just for amusement alone: the sexual organ of money,
everything, all of it, the process—, that is instructive
and yields fertility . . . . . . . . .
    . . . . Oh, but just beyond,

35  hinter der letzten Planke, beklebt mit Plakaten des "Todlos,"
    jenes bitteren Biers, das den Trinkenden süß scheint,
    wenn sie immer dazu frische Zerstreuungen kaun . . .,
    gleich im Rücken der Planke, gleich dahinter, ists *wirklich.*
    Kinder spielen, und Liebende halten einander,—abseits,
40  ernst, im ärmlichen Gras, und Hunde haben Natur.
    Weiter noch zieht es den Jüngling; vielleicht, daß er eine junge
    Klage liebt . . . . . Hinter ihr her kommt er in Wiesen. Sie sagt:
    —Weit. Wir wohnen dort draußen . . . .
                            Wo? Und der Jüngling
    folgt. Ihn rührt ihre Haltung. Die Schulter, der Hals—, vielleicht
45  ist sie von herrlicher Herkunft. Aber er läßt sie, kehrt um,
    wendet sich, winkt . . . Was solls? Sie ist eine Klage.

    Nur die jungen Toten, im ersten Zustand
    zeitlosen Gleichmuts, dem der Entwöhnung,
    folgen ihr liebend. Mädchen
50  wartet sie ab und befreundet sie. Zeigt ihnen leise,
    was sie an sich hat. Perlen des Leids und die feinen
    Schleier der Duldung.— Mit Jünglingen geht sie
    schweigend.

    Aber dort, wo sie wohnen, im Tal, der Älteren eine, der Klagen,
55  nimmt sich des Jünglinges an, wenn er fragt:— Wir waren,
    sagt sie, ein Großes Geschlecht, einmal, wir Klagen. Die Väter
    trieben den Bergbau dort in dem großen Gebirg; bei Menschen
    findest du manchmal ein Stück geschliffenes Ur-Leid
    oder, aus altem Vulkan, schlackig versteinerten Zorn.
60  Ja, das stammte von dort. Einst waren wir reich.—

    Und sie leitet ihn leicht durch die weite Landschaft der Klagen,
    zeigt ihm die Säulen der Tempel oder die Trümmer
    jener Burgen, von wo Klage-Fürsten das Land
    einstens weise beherrscht. Zeigt ihm die hohen
65  Tränenbäume und Felder blühender Wehmut,
    (Lebendige kennen sie nur als sanftes Blattwerk);
    zeigt ihm die Tiere der Trauer, weidend,—und manchmal
    schreckt ein Vogel und zieht, flach ihnen fliegend durchs Aufschaun,
    weithin das schriftliche Bild seines vereinsamten Schreis.—

behind the last planks, plastered with placards for "Deathless,"
that bitter beer which seems sweet to the drinkers
when they chew fresh distractions with it . . . ,
just beyond the planks, right behind them, it is *real*.
Children play and lovers embrace,—apart,
seriously, on the sparse grass, and dogs do what is natural.
The youth is attracted still farther; perhaps he loves a young
Lament . . . . . Following her he comes to meadows. She says:
—Far. We live out there . . . .
                Where? And the youth
follows. Her manner touches him. Her shoulder, her neck, perhaps
she is of noble descent. But he leaves her, turns back,
looks around, waves . . . What is the use? She is a Lament.

Only the youthful dead in the initial state
of timeless serenity, the state of becoming detached,
follow her lovingly. She waits
for girls and befriends them. Shows them gently
what she is wearing. Pearls of sorrow and the fine
veils of patience.—With youths she walks
in silence.

But where they live in the valley one of the older Laments
speaks with the youth when he asks:—We were,
she says, a great race once, we Laments. Our ancestors
engaged in mining there in the great mountain range; among men
you sometimes find a chunk of polished primeval pain
or cindery petrified anger from an old volcano.
Of course, it came from there. Once we were rich.—

And she guides him gently through the vast landscape of the
    Laments,
shows him the pillars of temples or the ruins
of those fortresses from which princes of Lament once
ruled the land wisely. Shows him the tall
tear trees and fields of flowering sadness,
(the living know it only as a delicate foliage);
shows him the cattle of mourning, grazing—, and sometimes
a bird starts up and flying low through their upward glance
draws in the distance the visible picture of its lonely cry.—

70 Abends führt sie ihn hin zu den Gräbern der Alten
aus dem Klage-Geschlecht, den Sibyllen und Warn-Herrn.
Naht aber Nacht, so wandeln sie leiser, und bald
mondets empor, das über Alles
wachende Grab-Mal. Brüderlich jenem am Nil,
75 der erhabene Sphinx—: der verschwiegenen Kammer
Antlitz.
Und sie staunen dem krönlichen Haupt, das für immer,
schweigend, der Menschen Gesicht
auf die Waage der Sterne gelegt.

80 Nicht erfaßt es sein Blick, im Frühtod
schwindelnd. Aber ihr Schaun,
hinter dem Pschent-Rand hervor, scheucht es die Eule. Und sie,
streifend im langsamen Abstrich die Wange entlang,
jene der reifesten Rundung,
85 zeichnet weich in das neue
Totengehör, über ein doppelt
aufgeschlagenes Blatt, den unbeschreiblichen Umriß.

Und höher, die Sterne. Neue. Die Sterne des Leidlands.
Langsam nennt sie die Klage: —Hier,
90 siehe: den *Reiter*, den *Stab*, und das vollere Sternbild
nennen sie: *Fruchtkranz*. Dann, weiter, dem Pol zu:
*Wiege; Weg; Das Brennende Buch; Puppe; Fenster.*
Aber im südlichen Himmel, rein wie im Innern
einer gesegneten Hand, das klar erglänzende "*M*,"
95 das die Mütter bedeutet . . . . . . —

Doch der Tote muß fort, und schweigend bringt ihn die ältere
Klage bis an die Talschlucht,
wo es schimmert im Mondschein:
die Quelle der Freude. In Ehrfurcht
100 nennt sie sie, sagt: —Bei den Menschen
ist sie ein tragender Strom. —

Stehn am Fuß des Gebirgs.
Und da umarmt sie ihn, weinend.

70 In the evening she takes him to the graves of past heroes
of the race of Lament, the sibyls and prophets.
As night approaches, however, they move more slowly, and soon
there rises up in the moonlight the monument
watching over everything. A brother to the one on the Nile,
75 the noble Sphinx—: the face of the silent
burial chamber.
And they gaze in wonder at the crowned head that has
silently placed the human countenance
on the scale of the stars forever.

80 Not that his sight comprehends it, still dizzy
from recent death. But her gaze startles an owl
from behind the double crown's edge. And it,
skimming slowly, brushing along the cheek,
the one with the fullest curve,
85 sketches lightly in the new
hearing of the dead, across the double
opened-out page, the indescribable outline.

And higher up, the stars. New ones. The stars of the Land of
Sorrow.
Slowly the Lament calls their names:—Here,
90 see: the *Rider*, the *Staff* and the larger constellation
they call: *Wreath of Fruit*. Then farther on toward the pole:
*Cradle, Road, The Burning Book, Puppet, Window.*
But in the southern sky, pure as the palm
of a hallowed hand, the clear sparkling "*M*"
95 which stands for Mothers . . . . . .—

But the dead youth must go on, and silently the older
Lament conducts him to the glen
where there sparkles in the moonlight:
the Spring of Joy. Reverently
100 she tells him its name, says:—in life
it is a navigable stream.—

They stand at the foot of the mountains.
And there she embraces him, weeping.

Einsam steigt er dahin, in die Berge des Ur-Leids.
105 Und nicht einmal sein Schritt klingt aus dem tonlosen Los.

Aber erweckten sie uns, die unendlich Toten, ein Gleichnis,
siehe, sie zeigten vielleicht auf die Kätzchen der leeren
Hasel, die hängenden, oder
meinten den Regen, der fällt auf dunkles Erdreich im Frühjahr. —

110 Und wir, die an *steigendes* Glück
denken, empfänden die Rührung,
die uns beinah bestürzt,
wenn ein Glückliches *fällt*.

Alone he climbs on, into the mountains of primeval sorrow.
105 And not even the sound of his step comes from the noiseless ground.

But if these infinitely dead ones awakened in us a comparison,
see, they would point perhaps to the hanging catkins
of the empty hazel or
would think of the rain which falls on the dark ground in
springtime.—

110 And we who think of *ascending*
good fortune, would experience the emotion
which almost overwhelms us
when something fortunate *falls*.

# COMMENTARY

# INTRODUCTION

The title of Rilke's *Duinesian Elegies* is derived from Castle Duino on the coast of the Adriatic Sea near Trieste, Italy. The ruins of what had once been a Roman watchtower and later a medieval castle where Dante wrote portions of the *Divine Comedy* stand atop white cliffs which plunge directly into the blue Adriatic. Back from the cliffs stands the castle where Rilke was staying in January 1912 when he began the elegies and wrote the first two of them and portions of the remaining ones. The castle was in the possession of the von Thurn und Taxis family at that time. Princess Marie von Thurn und Taxis-Hohenlohe, whom Rilke met in Paris in December 1909, was a friend and benefactor, and between 1910 and 1914 Rilke visited or stayed in this castle from time to time. It was during a long stay there from 22 October 1911 to 9 May 1912 that he was inspired to write the *Elegies* which have carried the name of the castle to many readers. Princess Marie von Thurn und Taxis-Hohenlohe tells in her memoirs that Rilke was walking along the parapet at the top of the cliffs in a strong wind pondering how to answer an annoying business letter when suddenly he seemed to hear in the wind a voice saying the opening line of the *Elegies*. He took out his notebook and wrote it down along with other lines which came without any effort, and by evening he had completed the first elegy.[1] Instead of formally dedicating the *Duinesian Elegies* to Princess Marie von Thurn und Taxis-Hohenlohe, Rilke introduces them as her "property."[2] The castle was greatly damaged during World War I, and Rilke inquired about its condition several times in his correspondence with the Princess.[3] It has since been restored by the family of von Thurn und Taxis to whom it still belongs.

The *Duinesian Elegies* are one of the great poetic achievements of all time and certainly are one of the greatest—if not the greatest—of the poetic works of the twentieth century. An inborn talent for poetic use of language sharpened by the conscious development of a craftsman-like precision as a result of his experience with the French sculptor, Auguste Rodin, produced

[1]Fürstin Marie von Thurn und Taxis-Hohenlohe, *Erinnerungen an Rainer Maria Rilke* (Frankfurt am Main: Insel, 1966), pp. 48–49.

[2]Rainer Maria Rilke, *Briefe* (Wiesbaden: Insel, 1950), II, 310.

[3]Rainer Maria Rilke, *Briefe aus den Jahren 1914 bis 1921* (Leipzig: Insel, 1938), pp. 45, 52–53, 66.

a poet with the rare combination of natural talent and careful discipline. Rilke had heard about Rodin from his wife, Clara Westhof-Rilke, a sculptress, and he met him when he wrote a monograph about the sculptor and his work in 1902. As Rodin's secretary from September 1905 to May 1906, Rilke learned careful and detailed observation, the value of conscious and continual application, patience, restraint, and control.[4] The poetic result of this association was the *New Poems*.

Even readers who do not comprehend fully the meaning of Rilke's works may sense their beauty. Complete appreciation requires that beyond intellectual comprehension the reader must react to their magnificence with an almost Buber-like I-Thou engagement. The beauty of these works leads the reader to desire to know them better, and the better one understands them, the more one appreciates their beauty and the genius of the author.

On an intellectual plane Rilke asks the age-old questions: what is man, what is the nature of his world, the universe, the absolute, and what is man's relationship to them. Man has been asking these questions for thousands of years; they are as old as man himself and rooted in man's awareness of himself. Self-awareness is one of the basic differences between man and animals, and each generation of man and each individual must ask these questions anew. They are the heart of what Albert Schweitzer calls basic thought, "gründliches Denken." This type of knowledge is not transmissible as fact, for its significance lies in the establishment of a living relationship between such thought and the individual—the meaning of such thought for life itself, not abstract knowledge. Ultimately each individual must find this relationship for himself, for it cannot be given to him. These questions are therefore essentially new for every thinker, writer, and reader who considers them. Although there are as many variations in such relationships as there are individuals to establish them, they may be divided broadly into two categories: the essentialist or idealistic orientation which starts with an abstract ideal or essence to which man compares himself, and the existentialist orientation which starts by asking what exists, what is the reality of life.

During the mid-nineteenth century the Danish philosopher, Søren Kierkegaard, published a number of philosophical works. In these works he departed radically from the accepted thinking of his time, and his writings

---

[4]K. A. J. Batterby, *Rilke and France* (London: Oxford University Press, 1966), p. 55.

remained almost completely unknown until the end of the nineteenth century. He sees man as basically imperfect and limited, due to his existing humanly, and therefore subject to finite freedom. He regards the world as fragmentary since man from his imprisonment within the world cannot view it objectively and as a whole. He views the absolute (God) as essentially unknowable to man, at least as factual information, and as an object of religious faith not demonstrable by proof. Rilke was familiar with the writings of Kierkegaard and learned Danish in order to read them and the works of the Danish novelist, Jens Peter Jacobsen, in the original language. He even translated some of Kierkegaard's letters to his betrothed, Regina Olsen, from Danish to German. Rilke's friend, the Austrian philosopher, Rudolf Kassner, to whom the eighth elegy is dedicated, was likewise interested in Kierkegaard as well as in eastern philosophy. Thus it is not surprising to find a basically existentialist orientation in Rilke's thought, although he lived and wrote prior to the publication of the major works in modern existentialism.

Like Kierkegaard, Rilke sees man as imperfect and limited, a situation rooted in the very fact of his existence. The painfulness of the human condition is further intensified by man's medial position between the animals and the absolute. Man has lost the blissful unawareness of the animals, yet he can only sense the existence of an absolute which he cannot know and which thereby becomes frustrating and terrible. Man's world is fragmented into two parts; firstly, the human sphere of life in time and space with all its problems and limitations; and secondly, the realm of the absolute (the angel or God), the home of perfection and eternity. A major problem in the Elegies then is the nature of the relationship between the parts of totality and what this implies for man.

Very briefly, Rilke's view is that man most nearly transcends himself and his world in love, when that love is itself an absolute and not the attraction of a specific object of love, which would itself be finite and passing. Art, too, presents us with a combination of the two worlds, the timely and the timeless, for it is the product of the human heart and its love and devotion, and man's path to the absolute is through his own absolute inner nature or heart. Complete disengagement can occur of course only in death. Man must find purpose and meaning in his own physical reality, not in some imagined realm of perfection or hereafter. In serving, preserving, and loving his own world, which is harmoniously coordinated with the absolute (the angel), he performs his own unique task within the universe. Because each of us is uniquely valuable and responsible for a unique task in the universe, we should praise life as meaningful and useful. Then even death becomes positive when viewed as a transition within a whole rather than as final end, a fall into totality rather than into nothingness. This is the message of Rilke's *Duinesian Elegies*, which begin with an anguished search for meaning in human life and end with a jubilant affirmation of life together with death as an inseparable part of life, as in the final images of hanging catkins and falling spring rain which combine connotations of awakening life with a falling curve symbolizing death.[5]

The elegies are structured around the fifth one as pivot. The preceding elegies stress the negative, limiting aspects of life, the following ones the positive, meaningful values. The fifth one balances the positive and negative aspects against each other as the acrobats perform feats of balance in their act. The transition occurs at the point where the angel approvingly accepts the smile of the acrobats, signifying man's value in the universe. Around this pivot the fourth elegy presents the subject–object division of the world as man sees it, balanced in the sixth by the view that when life and goal of life are identical, the divisions of life are sublimated into a higher unity. The third elegy balances the negative side of life as biological urge and emotional turmoil against love as the window through which external reality enters man's inner space in the seventh elegy. The second elegy presents the first major fracture in the universe as man sees it, into the realm of the angel and man's world of physical reality, a process which continues in the eighth elegy where physical reality is divided further into the spheres of man and creature. This division, however, is not painful like the first one, for it gives man a unique position in the universe, making him uniquely valuable. The first elegy states the major problems of the cycle, particularly the agonized inquiry whether man has any meaning in the universe, a question which is resolved in the ninth elegy where man is given the unique function of relating physical reality to the angel realm through his singular inner being. The tenth summarizes the entire cycle on the mythological level of the City of Grief and the Land of Lament.

[5]The basic approach to my interpretation of the *Duineser Elegien* is that applied in my dissertation, "Existentialist Thought in the Works of Rainer Maria Rilke" (University of Texas, 1958), *Dissertation Abstracts*, 19 (1958–59), 1750. The pattern of a totality fragmented into the worlds of man and angel I summarized and described in an article, "The Concept of Being in Rilke's *Elegien*," *Symposium*, 15 (1961), 12–21.

In addition to the pivotal structure around the fifth elegy, there are two sub-groups which balance each other. Sub-group A, the second, third, and fourth elegies, is devoted to human limitations: man's finite life in a world in which he is not at home, love as blind biological urge, and existence as a subject able to relate to his world solely as object. This group is balanced by sub-group B, the seventh, eighth, and ninth elegies, which shows that man's unique sphere of action is his own world where because of his self-aware-ness he consciously relates reality and the angel realm to each other. In this way he acquires a unique responsibility to his own world and finally finds his function and meaning in the universe. The structure of the elegies may be summarized by this diagram:

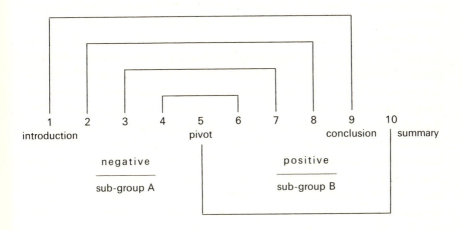

# THE FIRST ELEGY

The first elegy was composed in January 1912 in Castle Duino.[6] It opens
1   with the figure of the angel, which has received extensive critical treatment.
Rilke himself described the nature of the angel in a letter to Witold Hule-
wicz who translated the Elegies into Polish:

> The "angel" of the Elegies has nothing to do with the angel of the
> Christian heaven (more nearly with the angel figures of Islam) . . . The
> angel of the *Elegies* is that creation in which the transformation of the
> visible world into invisibility which we carry out appears already com-
> pleted. For the angel of the Elegies all earlier towers and bridges are
> existing, *because* they long have been invisible, and the still standing
> towers and bridges of our existence are *already* invisible, although (for
> us) still physically present. The angel of the Elegies is that being which
> stands for the idea of recognizing a higher order of reality in invisibility.[7]

The angel belongs to the absolute world of beauty, perfection, and
eternity. This realm of pure noncorporeal being is separated from the
human world of physical reality by a chasm unbridgeable for man and
angel alike. Although man intuitively senses the existence of this other realm
and longs for it, the angel cannot hear his cry, for the angel can perceive only
that which belongs to his own absolute world. Furthermore, there is no
place in our ordinary reality for the angel; if he were to enter our world, he
would destroy it, for he is not at home in it. Thus the angel which our long-
ing pictures as beauty becomes awesome or terrible, because he is and must
remain incomprehensible. Although beauty per se is an absolute concept,
we perceive it in our world as a function of physical reality. Thus we are
enabled to sense in the idea the existence of a pure absolute beyond our
awareness of beauty in reality, yet the experience remains painful because
we can never know beauty perfectly.[8] For man the universe remains insur-
mountably sundered because his very existence as a living creature impris-
oned within his existing body which he can escape only in death prevents
him from knowing directly the intangible perfection of the other world of
the angel.

---

[6]Rainer Maria Rilke, *Sämtliche Werke* (Frankfurt am Main: Insel, 1955), I, 873. All dates
of composition are taken from this source.

[7]Rilke, *Briefe*, II, 484. More of this letter is quoted in Appendix A, pp. 133–36.

[8]Else Buddeberg, *Die Duineser Elegien R. M. Rilkes* (Karlsruhe: Stahlberg, 1948), p. 5.

8      Recognition of the separation of these two realms means that man must renounce the temptation to call the angel, to lure him into the human world where he does not belong. There are areas of life where each individual must find his own answers—his relationship to the angel, to his own inner self, and to his world. These relationships are acquired by experience; they are not factual knowledge and therefore cannot be transmitted. In these areas neither man nor the angels can help or be of use to us. Each person must make his own life; he cannot escape that responsibility by transferring it to others such as the family or society or to some distant heavenly figure such as the angel.

11     The animals represent for Rilke a view of the world as unbounded unity in contrast to man's view of it as discrete. They sense that they are different, that man is insecure within his physical reality which he tries to arrange, master, and own, and on which he attempts to impose his concept of order. The animals who are innately one with the world—hence their view of it as a unity—sense that in trying to possess the world as object, man has lost his secure position within reality without acquiring the ability to escape from his imprisonment within it. What then is left for man? Is anything securely his? There remains only his inner reality, only that which has been transformed into inner permanence—some repeatedly seen view such as a tree or some action which through continually repeated use has become part of us as habit. Nothing except what has become an integral part of our enduring inner being can belong securely to us.

8      For Rilke, lovers represent man's most successful attempt to escape himself—to transcend his limitations. This is symbolized by the wind of outer space which tears at our faces in the night. At night we do not see so clearly as in the day; we are more nearly one with our world. Because we cannot see where it ends, it is vaster. We are more open to the other world of the angel, closer to it, and it is closer to us. It feeds on our faces and forces upon us the painfully troublesome task of understanding ourselves and our universe. Night is also the time for lovers, and Rilke inquires if the task of understanding is easier for them. His answer is negative. Even they cannot escape from themselves, and even if they could, the other would still block the view. They are no more securely at home in this world than everyone else. The distance from one human being to another—even the beloved—is insurmountable. Each embrace remains empty since the individual cannot find himself in another. When we truly comprehend this, we are again

confronted with the question of what is left for us, what our task and our meaning are, and once more we are referred to inner reality. The past, beauty and art in the symbol of the violin, and the things of our world need us. It is our responsibility to perceive and transform them into enduring form within us. But we are distracted continually from this basic task by constantly changing cares, needs, and desires, by short-range goals and ties to others. Rilke sometimes summarizes all these distractions with one word—destiny.

33      Although one person cannot shelter or protect another nor find shelter in another even in the most intense love, love remains one of the most positive actions man can perform. This positive aspect is the act of love itself, not that one loves this or that object, but that one *loves*. The significance then is for the one who loves—the giver, not for the one who is loved—a passive receiver. The loss of a loved one through either death or desertion may thus have the positive aspect of freeing love from an object with corresponding transformation into an absolute. For Rilke this is the signi-

46      ficance of the Italian poetess, Gaspara Stampa (1523–1554), who captured her love in poetry of genuine passion and expressive power. In a letter to Annette Kolb dated 23 January 1912,[9] he wrote that he considered three women, Gaspara Stampa, Louize Labé, and Marianna Alcoforado, the most nearly perfect examples of unrequited love as a positive force. It is significant that all three examples of such near-perfect love are women, for Rilke believed that woman was capable of loving more freely and less demandingly than man. The acceptance of such lovers back into nature

43      signifies the value of their act. In transforming their love into an absolute, it became a springboard for self-transcendence wherein they overcame their separation from the world and reached a state of harmonious oneness with nature. Thus their lives, like the lives of heroes, mirror in their unity of purpose the harmonious perfection of the universe. The impetus of such love does for life what the bowstring does for the arrow: it frees us from the limitations of the here and now for the absolute world of the angel. In transcending ourselves, we become more than ourselves, as the arrow becomes more than itself in flight.

54      The beginning of the next section, "voices, voices," signifies a major change in theme. We are given the task of listening as saints formerly

[9]Rilke, *Briefe*, I, 344–48.

74

listened to the voice of God, so completely that the world of reality fell away and they were aware of God's voice alone. But their world is no longer ours, and modern man could not endure God's voice. We hear "das Wehende," an indefinable wafting, afflatus, or the breath of God if Christian terminology were possible here, something which exists, yet has no form. It stands for our responsibility to rescue the vanishing object world into our own enduring inner being. This wafting carries a message of silence. Such silence is not the absence of sound; it stands for perfect harmony. In the *Sonnets to Orpheus* man hears or listens to the song of Orpheus. The accoustical level of noise is comparable to the finite world of man in the Elegies. The absolute world of the angel corresponds to the accoustical form of harmony, and ultimate harmony is silence. Silence therefore signifies a view of the universe as totality where life and death are merely parts of a whole as the child sees it, a view which man senses but can know perfectly only in death. Santa Maria Formosa is a small church in Venice which Rilke visited with Princess Marie von Thurn und Taxis-Hohenlohe. The tablet is thought to be one with a Latin inscription located near the right side altar.[10]

Such silence speaks of the relationship between life and death. What meaning does the death of a young person or a child hold for us? We are accustomed to say that it is unfortunate, that their life still lay before them. Rilke tells us that this is incorrect, that we do them an injustice. Our view from the life side of totality is distorted; and in trying to hold back those who die by viewing them as still one of us, we hinder them, limit their freedom. From the death side of totality their view is different. The physical reality of earth is no longer significant and the customs they learned there are useless. Since they are now in the angel's world of eternity, time with its emphasis on the future and on duration falls away, as would the human connotation of good fortune and long life for roses.[11] In this other realm the child is perfectly free, no longer subject to having his life made for him by others—by family, relatives, and all those who infringe on his life by trying to shape it in their image. Even his name, his mark of earthly uniqueness, falls away. The dead have no wishes, for they have no future and no needs.

[10]Romano Guardini, *Rainer Maria Rilkes Deutung des Daseins* (Munich: Kösel, 1953), pp. 61–62.

[11]Jacob Steiner, *Rilkes Duineser Elegien* (Bern and Munich: Francke, 1962), pp. 31–32.

All the things of this world have no meaning in the other realm where they only flap loosely and uselessly. Only man separates the living from the dead; the angel sees the dead as part of the stream of eternity. In both the English translation and the German original the reference to "those of all ages" means young and old and those who have lived throughout the existence of the human race.

Rilke views the universe as dynamic, not static. The realm of the dead is filled with dynamic change, just as our own world is. Only the total configuration remains sustained by the dynamic change within. As in Goethe's heaven in *Faust*, the dead of the Elegies continue to change, adapting gradually to their new condition. The living alone distinguish sharply between the living and the dead; in viewing the world as a harmonious unity, the angel is unaware of the chasm which for us divides the universe.

86 In the end those who die young do not need us; our world no longer has any meaning for them. It is we who need them.[12] We need their message that life and death are integrated parts of a great totality, a message of comfort and help for us.

91 The theme of life and death as a harmonious unity and the theme of accoustical or musical harmony are linked in the legend of Linos which closes this elegy. There are several legends concerning Linos, and in all of them he is linked with Apollo, the god of song. According to some legends he was either the brother or son of Apollo, according to others he was killed by Apollo who was jealous of his musical talent. In all of the legends he was musically talented and died young, a combination which Rilke found significant. He used it to close this elegy as a symbol demonstrating that man's ultimate limitation, death, is part of a harmonious totality where it loses the sharp finality which it customarily holds for man.

The first elegy presents all the major themes of the entire cycle. It inquires about the nature of man, the angel, and the world, and about man's relationship to himself, to the transcendental realm of the angel, and to his own world. Love is presented as man's springboard for self-transcendence. Lovers and heroes signify in their unity of purpose a view of the cosmos as undivided whole. We alone are separated from our surrounding world; for the animal, the child, and the angel life has never lost its primal unity. These symbols will continue to appear in the elegies, pointing the way to a view of our own world as coordinated with the absolute world of the angel in a meaningful universe.

[12]Buddeberg, p. 19.

# THE SECOND ELEGY

The second elegy was written at Castle Duino in January and February 1912. It focuses on the nature of the angel, the nature of man and the relationship between them.[13] The angels, which open this elegy, are described as "near fatal birds of the soul," calling to mind the traditional pictures of them as winged creatures. The description overlaps the traditional view of the angels as heavenly beings and thus creatures of the soul and Rilke's own complex symbol of the bird as belonging to both the world of man as a living thing and to the realm of the angel as a creature of air and space and in its oneness with its surroundings.[14] The deadliness or menace which the angel represents for our human world recalls the description of the angel in the first elegy. The angel with his celestial perfection is unaware of our world of material reality and would destroy it if he tried to enter it. This means that Rilke's angel differs from the angel of the Judeo-Christian tradition as demonstrated in the story of Tobias in the apocryphal Book of Tobit. According to this story the archangel Raphael came down to earth and assumed the form of a young man to act as a guide for Tobias when he was sent to Media to bring back funds left there by his father.[15] But, says Rilke, the days when an angel could enter our world disguised as one of us have gone forever. Now we would perish if the angel were to approach our world by just one step. The human and the angel worlds are separated by an abyss which cannot be bridged directly, so that the angel no longer can function as a messenger between man and transcendence.

The second section of the second elegy is one of the most lyrical passages in the entire cycle. Although the angels are not part of our world, Rilke tries to capture their essence in these lines where their beauty is reflected in the lyrical beauty of their description. In their perfection they are the acme of creation. As first creations in both time and degree of significance they stand for eternity, for time without beginning, change, and end, but like the rest of the universe they are creations, not God the creator.[16] Their existence is perfect harmony, as is nature in the mountain ranges and dawn-

---

[13]This theme is treated extensively in E. P. Isler, "La structure des Elégies de Duino de Rainer Maria Rilke," *Les langues modernes*, 35 (1937), 226–30.

[14]Buddeberg, p. 23.

[15]Steiner, pp. 38–39.

[16]Heinrich Kreutz, *Rilkes Duineser Elegien* (Munich: C. H. Beck, 1950), p. 39.

reddened peaks. Moving from the light of dawn, the angels are envisioned as pure light, junctures of light with intersecting rays, avenues of light, and staircases of light rising to thrones of light, which returns to the beginning of the section where the angels are the crowning glory of creation. The circular construction symbolizes the never-ending dynamism of radiation and reconcentration of light in the final lines of this section. Angels traditionally have been described as radiant; these angels are light itself. Light in the angel world corresponds to water in our own human world. Both light and flowing water are dynamic, not static. Both appear to remain unchanged and enduring, yet both are formed of a dynamic and continually changing stream or beam. Both therefore symbolize an unchanging totality sustained by the dynamics of continual change. The additional elements of essence, ecstasy, and emotion are likewise dynamic and non-tangible. The final picture of the angels as mirrors radiating light and beauty and reconcentrating it again repeats and sharpens the image of infinitely, blindingly brilliant beings unchanging in their tempestuously dynamic existence.[17] In earlier writings Rilke used the image in the mirror symbolically to represent the inner world, in contrast to external reality before the mirror as in the Christine Brahe episode in *Malte Laurids Brigge*. Since the angels are themselves mirrors, they stand for perfect unity of inner and outer images as opposed to man's divided world.

This interpretation disagrees with Guardini's statement that the angels are no longer messengers of God, but have been transformed into earthly creatures.[18] As he points out, Rilke's angel is not the angel of revelation, nor a messenger between man and God. But instead of the distance between man and the angel decreasing as it would if the angel were drawn into the human world, it has increased until it has become insurmountable. For man this means that his world is hopelessly fragmented. At best he can surmise tentatively a unity which he can never know fully except in death.

18 The third section turns to the contrasting picture of man dominated by his mortality, his transitoriness. Man is compared to glowing embers which gradually vanish as the odor they emit fades away. Ernst Zinn informs us that this passage alludes to the burning of amber or sweetgum wood as incense.[19] In the absolute world of the angel nothing is lost in the emanation

[17]Steiner, p. 43. The dynamic character of the absolute also appears in my dissertation.
[18]Guardini, p. 73.
[19]Ernst Zinn, "Nachwort des Herausgebers," *Rainer Maria Rilkes Sämtliche Werke*, I, 792.

and reconcentration of essence, but man belongs to the material world where all that is emanated is lost forever.[20] Not even in the fiery emotion of love can human beings find shelter or permanence. The others, the loved ones, perish like everyone else. The world we live in is no more permanent than we ourselves are. Although our houses and all the things we make and build seem to outlast us, they exist as we do in time and space and also perish. Nature itself which appears enduring is continually changing, even if according to predictable cycles. Everything which has substance is subject to change; we can find no shelter, permanence, or protection in the world of physical reality. No amount of love can restrain us or others; youth and beauty inevitably forsake us. Not even love can alter the fact that we are living creatures doomed to death. What then is the significance of human life? Do we have any meaning in the universe, any relationship to the angel realm? Once again, the answer is negative. The angel is incapable of perceiving man's world of physical reality; he is at home only in his own world. If he tried to enter our world he would destroy it, and our world can enter the angel world only as essence, not as physical reality. The two spheres must remain eternally separated, and man's comprehension of the universe necessarily remains fragmentary.

The first elegy found love one of man's most positive actions, and once again Rilke turns to lovers in his search for meaning. Like trees and houses, like all the physical world except for man, lovers, if they knew how, could tell us why they and this world seems more permanent, more durable than we ourselves. How can this be? The previous section has just pointed out that everything in our world and our very world itself is just as subject to change and destruction as we ourselves are. We, however, differ from the rest of our world in one important respect—we are aware of our impermanence and separated from our world by a subject-object barrier so that we know it only as object. Where the world of things and animals simply exists in harmonious unity, man with his unique awareness of himself and his world consciously seeks knowledge and security even though his very separation from his world as subject renders this ultimately impossible. The things and animals cannot or do not explain why this is so. Perhaps this is because they do not understand it; understanding is peculiarly human. Perhaps it is because they are ashamed for us that we have withdrawn from their world of innate unity. Yet in withdrawing from their world we have

[20]Buddeberg, p. 28.

opened up new modes of life, and perhaps we have opened up new possibilities corresponding to our new way of life for the rest of physical reality as well as for ourselves. Therefore we also represent hope for the world of creatures. The later elegies will define one such new possibility, but that is better left for later.

*44*     If anyone can transcend himself and the inborn limitations of human life, it is the lover. Lovers draw strength from each other. Does this tell us something about them and about ourselves? As they touch each other, so we touch ourselves; we fold our hands or rest our tired face within them. But this proves only that we exist physically in time and space. Lovers seek and believe they find more than this in their love; they promise themselves enduring love, pure permanence, and eternity. They *almost* achieve these goals; they attain so much, yet they are doomed to fall short because they are inalterably imprisoned within their human form. They, their love, and their world undergo change like everything else. Even the unique and in-
*60* comparable experience of first love is subject to the progression of time. After the first glances, the longing for the loved one, the first innocent pleasures of being together, even lovers change. At the end of their experience they are not the same people they were at the beginning. Love furthermore conceals the danger that instead of transcending themselves, each other, and their world and thereby finding their unchanging essence, they lose themselves in the emotional tumult. Instead of finding freedom in love—symbolized by the window as opening to transcendence—they fall victim to their own emotions and drives and become playthings of events rather than their masters. The significance of love lies in its meaning for the one who loves; one can find only himself in love, not another.

*66*     In the next to the last section Rilke turns to the past and inquires if man has always been so alone. Were the Greeks with their greater gift for moderation more fortunate than modern man? The question combines the themes of love and farewell. An answer is sought in the portrayal of parting on Grecian stelé or gravestones where the living lay their hands on the dead who are represented as veiled and with bowed heads. Farewell may imply mere parting, but since it is the farewell depicted on Grecian gravestones, the final parting of death dominates the picture. If the concept of grief which was developed in the "Requiem für Wolf Graf von Kalckreuth" is considered, the milder expression of love and parting on the Grecian tombs indicates a greater feeling of identity with the totality of Being, with the concept of life and death as an inseparable unity. But since modern man has lost this feeling of oneness with *both* worlds, the sharpness of loss in death is intensified for him. It is his task and his responsibility to proceed under these altered conditions. Since even lovers are human, parting is inevitably linked to love, either through change in human relationships or through death. But since it is only the object of love which vanishes, love itself endures if it is absolute and not linked to an object. This is the positive message of the gentler farewells on the Grecian memorial shafts.

4     The final section draws together and summarizes the second elegy. The human limitations expressed so poignantly beginning with the third section are implied in the conditional form of the beginning of this last section: if only we, too, could find . . . a strip of fertile soil. Taking into account the nature of human life, man needs to find his purpose in this world. Too often he is caught up in the whirlwind of emotion and carried along by it as by a stream, or else he seeks to impose order and permanence on his world, to make it as static and unchanging as the rocks.[21] Man needs to find something characteristically human, meaningful, and attainable between these two extremes, a fertile soil where he can make his own unique contribution to the universe. But being human, he reaches too high and demands the perfection of the angel world rather than searching for significance within his own. Modern man has lost the Greek ideal of moderation as embodied in their art. It is his heartache that he senses what he cannot know and demands the unattainable. In reaching for what is beyond his grasp and rejecting the limitations of his own world, he is left without home or meaning.

[21]Buddeberg, p. 37.

The third elegy was begun at Duino in 1912 and expanded and completed in Paris in the late autumn of 1913. It is devoted to the theme of love and uses psycho-analytical terminology as a tool for examining it. In the German it is clear that the loved one in the opening line refers to a girl or woman (grammatically it is feminine), so that the perspective of the

4 opening section is masculine. Here the term "loved one" is not a negative contrast to the action of loving, but represents in the pure love of woman the positive aspect of love. The brief opening reference to woman's love is immediately drowned out by the appearance of masculine love with its instinctive urges in the mythical figure of Neptune. As the riverine god he is related to the stream which bounds one side of the fertile soil sought by man in the closing lines of the second elegy and thereby related also to man's loss of freedom in complete surrender to his physical and emotional drives. As god of streams, Neptune is also god of the blood stream and thus stands for man's physical inheritance. His love opens the way to the chaos of

9 tumult, the uproar of uncontrolled passion. The wind of his conch is the dark call of chaos and confusion. It is unrelated to the winds of space which devour our faces in the night in the first elegy, for those winds come from the ordered angel realm. The closing lines of the first section return to the opening theme of praise for woman's love. They inquire whether, in spite

12 of the dark side of love, it is not related to the pure, vast, unchanging world of the stars, whether through the possibility of his love for woman, man may be led to her purer love.

14 The second section portrays the function of woman as mother and as beloved in bringing order and meaningfulness into the masculine world. To accomplish this, however, the woman must contend with the unconscious level of instinct inherited along with physical form, which compels the man to act in ways he does not understand. For him the call of the instinctive urge and the yearning for ideal, nurturing love are inextricably bound together. When a girl awakens love in a youth, she awakens simultaneously its dark erotic tumult which agitates and convulses him. Although the youth himself may desire to escape this sinister aspect of love, he cannot succeed completely; he is forever bound to his reality as an existing being.

26 The mother's task appears easier than that of the beloved; she is able to do much for the child. She not only creates the child physically, she makes his

world for him; and the world she creates appears friendly, ordered, and harmless. Her figure, slender like the figure of a girl, shuts out the other realm of darkness, destiny, and chaos. She can explain everything to the child—temporarily, at least—and when she gets up at night, the unknown retreats before her presence like darkness before a nightlight. But she cannot eliminate his inborn world; it merely retreats as far as the wardrobe or the curtains, waiting for her to leave to reassert its presence. In spite of her great powers, her accomplishments are limited. There are areas which lie beyond her reach. There she can be of no use to the youth, for not even the mother can alter the given nature of human life.

The third section contrasts the apparent order of the external world which the mother creates for the child with the chaos of his inherited inner world. Although outwardly the child appears protected, his inner world is defenseless, for external sheltering cannot extend into the inner area of inheritance. The inner world of the third elegy differs from the inner world of the remaining elegies where it is linked to the realm of the angels. Here it stands for the inborn erotic aspect of love and its compulsive emotional turmoil symbolized by the primeval forest with its choking underbrush and grasping tendrils where the pale green of the new growth of the young man's heart springs from the fallen trees of the dead of earlier generations.[22] In this world eternity is achieved through procreation, through Dionysian perpetuation of the race, and the individual is significant only as a link in the chain, not for himself alone. The birth of the individual—his own little birth—is a subordinate part of the line of succession, whose maintenance justifies the horror and suffering inflicted by the pitiless demands of love as biological urge. Yet this aspect of love is so much a part of man's heritage that it seems friendly and not at all terrible, deceiving him into complacency and acceptance. He is, after all, a product of the procreative chain, and his inherited nature was part of him even before he was born.

The flowers of the fourth section stand for the simple harmony of reproduction in nature and signify a return to the contrasting purity and unselfishness of woman's love which is free to love for the sake of love alone, free from the compulsion of the chain of procreation. When the man loves, his love is bound to the past and to the future and includes those who have preceded and those who will follow. He alone cannot love the maiden, for

[22]Steiner, pp. 61–62.

his predecessors and his successors are inexorably present in his love, and he does not love her alone, for he loves all those others, too. This is human destiny—all those factors which are an inherent part of man and his existence as an entity in time and space. These factors are present even before they are awakened by the girl's love, and she cannot avoid arousing them.

76    The last section continues the contrast between masculine and feminine love from the preceding one. What is the woman to do since her love awakens relentless biological drives in man? The answer to this question is the positive hope which is the message of this elegy. By her own free, undemanding love, she is able to bring order, freedom, and peace into the man's tumultuous world. Her love is able to transform the wilderness of his uncontrolled passion into the ordered, productive beauty of a garden. It counterbalances his heritage and makes love a meaningful and fulfilling element in life by showing him how to love so that the heart, in opening to accept the loved one, remains open for the whole world. The final "hold

84    him" gathers together all the meanings of love. The German "verhalten" means to hold back or restrain, and refers to the counterbalance which the woman provides to man's heritage. If the first letter of the word is removed, the word, "erhalten," remains, which means to sustain, to hold up, to keep, to nourish, and this, too, is part of woman's dependable labor of love. The word furthermore contains the stem, "halten," which can mean to hold or embrace, and this is likewise part of the service of love for both the mother and the loved one.[23]

Woman's love, like the strip of fertile soil in the second elegy, points a way to a positive area in human life where man may find and fulfill his purpose in his own real world. In reaching the outermost limits of that world in love, he very nearly transcends himself in an action which in its purest form escapes the limits of time and space to become an unbounded absolute related to the stars and the angel.

[23]Professor Allan W. Anderson, a colleague in the Department of Religious Studies, has informed me that this thought configuration is also present in hexagram 26, "The Taming Power of the Great," where the three aspects of "holding firm" are (1) holding together, (2) holding back and (3) nourishing. *I Ching or Book of Changes*, trans. C. F. Baynes and R. Wilhelm (Princeton: Princeton University Press, 1967), p. 104.

# THE FOURTH ELEGY

The fourth elegy was written 22 and 23 November 1915 in Munich. The dominant theme is man's knowledge that he must die, which forces him to view life and death as mutually exclusive opposites in contrast to the undivided oneness of life as the creature world experiences it. The second, third, and fourth elegies form a structural unit devoted to man's view of life and the universe as fractured into irreconcilable parts. The second elegy divides the universe into the spheres of man and angel; the third divides love into the inherited biological drive of man and the pure, unselfish love of woman; and the fourth divides the mature view of life and death as a duality, with death as final end from the creature view of life and death as a harmonious unity with death as transformation. The fourth elegy stresses awareness of death as limitation, continuing the theme of man as limited being from the two preceding elegies.

1     In the opening line life is described as a tree. The tree passes through the cycles of the seasons without prior awareness of change because it is one with nature; and like the real tree, the tree of life has its natural cycles. Man, however, differs from the tree and from the rest of nature because he alone is aware of death. This awareness turns his view backward since death acts like a wall, shutting off his view of what lies beyond and forcing him to see life and death as opposites. Thus we are not in accord, not of one mind, or as the first elegy states, we are not at home in our world. From our position within the whole but separated from it by a subject-object barrier, we are always faced with Kierkegaardian either-or choices without sufficient knowledge to foresee clearly the consequences. Unlike nature, we ourselves are involved in making our seasons. We make bad choices, or as in the picture of the migrating birds, we make our choices at the wrong time so that our passage may be hindered by wintry winds. For the trees and birds, the coming of winter is another natural season in an ever-recurring cycle, for they share the concept of late fall or winter as a period of dormancy followed by rebirth. For man, however, winter implies death, as in the statement, "We are simultaneously aware of flourishing and withering." The animals such as the lion, in contrast, are unaware of death; they exist in simple harmony since their view is not limited.

The second section begins with a restatement and enlargement of the theme that man, unlike the animals, knows both life and death. The animals thus view life as a rising curve, where man sees it as a falling curve. Even lovers, who can almost promise themselves eternity in the second elegy, must ultimately face the fact that they are mortal and perish like everyone else. Instead of freedom and openness in love, they find limitations, instead of chase possession, and instead of sanctuary insecurity.[24] But Rilke reminds us that lovers nevertheless reach the outermost limits of life, and in the act of love are nearer to transcending life's limitations than are other human beings.

14    The second part of the second section stresses the significance for others of the limitation of death for lovers. Like contrasting background in a painting, the existence of this limitation forces others to view the lovers sharply and clearly as physical beings. They appear before us with the clarity of external reality where death is a fact understandable as outside stimulus. Others do not learn from the experience of lovers because their message is not factual information but must be learned by each individual for himself. Lovers are deflected back by their mortality from the outermost reaches of love into the harsh world of time and space where their message cannot be shared. The contours of their emotion are doomed to remain unfamiliar to all except themselves.

19    The third portion of the second section turns from the picture of life as a tree to life as a stage where the players are one's inner being or heart, emphasizing man's unique awareness of himself. The scenery, the backdrop for life, is farewell—man's mortality. Against this background the ordinary person and his claim to a full life appear as mere pretensions, for he cannot escape the conflicting ties and relationships of his world. The garden, which in the previous elegy was a symbol for order and meaningfulness, is here only a backdrop, a two-dimensional false and deceptive order imposed by man. In appearing as a dancer, man demonstrates his physical virtuosity which is a prominent theme in the fifth elegy. This dancer does not transmit meaning; he goes through the motions of life without comprehending its nature or significance. Except for his role as dancer, he is like everyone else when he is not performing; his life is a hollow role.[25]

26    The fourth and final section of the second stanza rejects life as an empty virtuoso performance without inner significance. The dancer is replaced by

[24]Kreutz, p. 61.
[25]Kreutz, p. 63.

the figure of the doll or puppet or marionette—the German word can mean all three. The wire indicates a marionette, but the distinction is probably not vital. It is an object, a thing, without mind or soul. Its nature is completely external, and this figure represents man as physical reality.[26] In an essay written early in 1914, Rilke describes the function of the doll for the child. He says that the child does not see the doll or puppet as a physical thing alone, but something more—an invisible soul—which is above both the puppet and the child.[27] The child then grows through the distance which separates the inanimate object from the soul above and acquires its own soul—inner being—by doing so. This is the positive value of the doll or marionette as it appears in an elegy fragment in 1913–1914:

> Oh doll,
> most distant figure—, as stars grow through distance
> into worlds, you make the child into a star.
> If physical space is too small for it: you spread out
> between you spaces of feeling, more intense space.[28]

The stage of the heart is occupied by man as an existing physical phenomenon. Rather than the half-filled delusions of the dancer, it is at least filled with reality. The spectator waits patiently before the inner stage for a performance which will reveal more than this reality, reminding the reader of the closing lines of the requiem, "Für Wolf Graf von Kalckreuth," with their statement that perseverance is at the heart of life. Man must persevere and endure life, continuing to hope for sudden change to meaningfulness. The spectator continues to wait, even when only emptiness comes from the stage, when he cannot see beyond the confines of reality and the world appears limited, cold, and meaningless. He continues to wait even when the woman and the child—those closer to the angel world than anyone else— have left. The description of the child with the immobile brown eye reminds us of Erik Brahe in *Malte Laurids Brigge*. There, too, he was at home in both the world of the living and the world of the dead, as his eyes indicate. The lively brown eye belongs to the real world of the living, and the unmoving eye stands for the unchanging world of the dead and the angel.[29]

[26]Rilke, *Briefe*, I, 345.
[27]Rilke, *Sämtliche Werke*, VI, 1070.
[28]Rilke, *Sämtliche Werke*, II, 459. My own translation.
[29]Steiner, p. 83.

The emptiness of the stage from which the gray draft comes stands for death and implies a way of life overshadowed by awareness of death.[30] It recalls the ninth sonnet of the first cycle of the *Sonnets to Orpheus* where we are reminded that only he who can sing praise even in full knowledge of the limitation of death can truly acknowledge and praise life. In this elegy likewise man experiences life fully and recognizes beyond its limitations its link to the absolute world of the angel when he faces death in the complete aloneness inherent in the human condition.

37    The third section inquires into the meaning which the finality of human life has for those who love—father, family, friends, or lovers. All of them try to make the child or loved one into their image of him. This limits the freedom and hinders the free development of the object of love, which is a dominant theme in Rilke's version of the parable of the prodigal son. Rilke's own experience is reflected here, for his father planned a military career for him and was greatly puzzled by his son's so very different talents and inclinations.[31] The son of this section does not love as he is loved. His

50    love does not depend on specific individuals as objects of love, but transcends them to become an absolute existing independently of the object of love. It is purely spiritual love which leaves its object free, points the way to self-transcendence, and is free from the limitations of life. Such love is man's link to the angel world of the absolute. In response to it the angel

55    comes and animates the puppet on the stage of the heart. Together puppet and angel become a paradoxical unity of the incomplete reality of mortal man and absolute reality, of immanence and transcendence, as comple-

61    mentary parts of a meaningful whole. Note that the angel performs *above* the puppet. The worlds of man and angel remain separated but coordinated. In his heart man transcends his existence as subject separated from all other objects and relates to the grand totality of the universe. In this action his function and meaning are revealed to him; he understands that he has a vital role to play, even though it is limited by physical reality and doomed by death. He sees the seasons of his own life as part of a complete universal cycle. Those approaching the end of life and the child at the beginning of life are nearer to such a view than others. The child has not outgrown his

---

[30]E. L. Stahl, "Introduction," *Rainer Maria Rilke's Duineser Elegien* (Oxford: Basil Blackwell, 1965), pp. xiv–xv.

[31]Guardini, p. 155.

innate unity with nature, and the dying see beyond the subject-object limitation to a regained oneness with totality. The view from the beginning and the end of life thus differs from that of the mature individual. The child's oneness with nature is characterized by a time concept different from that of the mature person for whom time is a continuum of past, present, and future. The child does not distinguish so sharply; he is content to live intensely in the present moment, unaware of the passage of time, satisfied with things of the spirit, and endowing the whole world with permanence since he is unaware of impermanence. He stands as a link between the world of man and the world of the angel in his innate harmony with the universe and in his unawareness of death which he shares with the animals. Although the child must grow up, must outgrow this pleasant harmony, the memory remains to point the way to the possibility that such a condition may exist again.

The final section summarizes the message of the fourth elegy in the figure of the child. The wonder and mysterious significance of childhood are suggested in the opening question, who can possibly understand childhood, and again in the closing statement that childhood is inexpressible. The role of childhood as one of the great positive possibilities of life is demonstrated by its position as a star in the firmament of life, for the stars belong to the absolute world of the angel. The measuring rod of distance in the hand of the child could measure two distances—the distance of the child from the limited, divided world of the mature individual, and the distance through which the child grows to reach the angel world which he senses above him and the doll. Yet even the child with his unawareness of death as final limit bears within himself death, though not like the ordinary person. In the child, death is a fruit, a theme which occurred in *The Book of Hours* and in *Malte Laurides Brigge*. Death is an inborn and inseparable part of life, an organic part of human development, not something imposed as end from without. For the mature individual who sees life and death as opposing poles rather than as harmonious parts of a whole, this is almost impossible to comprehend. Even the horror of murder is easier to understand, and the mature person usually regards death as murder, as an arbitrary and undesirable end imposed from without. The positive message of this elegy in the figure of the child is that this is an error, that life and death are harmonious parts of a greater whole, and that death is to be accepted unquestioningly as the child accepts it.

Pablo Picasso: *Family of Saltimbanques*
NATIONAL GALLERY OF ART, WASHINGTON
CHESTER DALE COLLECTION

## THE FIFTH ELEGY

The fifth elegy was written 14 February 1922 after all the others had been completed. It is dedicated to Mrs. Hertha Koenig, who was the owner of the 1905 painting by Picasso, *La famille des saltimbanques*. Rilke had been familiar with the painting even before Mrs. Koenig acquired it, and from mid-June to mid-October 1915 he stayed in her apartment in Munich where the painting hung.[32] Also contributing to the background of this elegy is Rilke's description of a performance by the well-known acrobatic troupe of Père Rollin in Paris in a letter dated 14 July 1907.[33]

Like the doll of the fourth elegy, the acrobats represent the physical reality of human life. In contrast to the actor whose role may have meaning

[32]Steiner, p. 101.

[33]Dieter Bassermann, *Der späte Rilke* (Munich: Leibniz, 1947), p. 415. See Appendix B, p. 137.

or to the dancer whose motions may convey an idea, the acrobats present physical virtuosity without inner reference or meaning. Their significance for the elegies lies in the nature of their lives—their complete rootlessness and insecurity. The fifth elegy is possibly the most complex of all the elegies in its symbolism and meaning, and the element of physical virtuosity has both positive and negative aspects. To the extent that an absence of inner or absolute reality is implied, it is negative; but complete and willing acceptance of the physical reality of life together with all its suffering and limitations is a positive element.

*1*     In these acrobats the transitoriness of human life is illuminated even more clearly than in those who partially hide from its impermanence in more permanent elements such as home, family, and work. The rootlessness of the acrobats causes the fleeting quality of their lives and all human life to stand out more sharply.[34] They stand for all the limitations which physical existence imposes on man, for their lives function on this level alone. They are mere objects, subject to the whims and changes of the moment, without continuity, and driven by the outward purpose of perfecting their performance. Their lives are like their acrobatic performances—in life they are twisted, bent, pitched, and thrown by external circumstances just as they are in their act.

This is a wandering acrobatic troupe without tent or protection from the forces of nature. Their stage is the carpet which they spread out, a carpet worn thin by continual usage. Translated to the level of human life, our lives are a performance on some worn carpet, some insignificant spot lost in the vastness of the universe. These acrobats do not perform in the rich suburbs or the center of town, but in the poorer areas at the edge of town where town and country meet and where the nature which survives is scrubby and wounded and scarred by the encroachment of the town.[35] Their performance temporarily covers over the harsh reality of life in such a place and presents in its stead the semblance of perfection like a bandage over a wound.

As soon as the acrobats arrive wherever they are to perform, they are on exhibit, even while setting up and practicing. The lines beginning with "And scarcely there," are among the most difficult in all the elegies to

[34]Guardini, p. 187.
[35]Guardini, pp. 189–90.

14  translate. The German speaks of the capital letter of "Dastehen," and the capital "D" refers not only to the role of the capital letter and the role of the word itself but also to the triangular composition of the Picasso painting. Unfortunately there is no good English translation which retains the compactness and plasticity of the German and begins with the initial "D." The best possible solution appears to be to expand to two words which capture the double significance of the acrobatic symbolism—the positive aspect of man's patient endurance of the trials of life while exposed to its negative limitations in complete defenselessness. The only other possibility would be"diligence," which touches the more positive aspects of the German but misses the negative ones. In speaking of the capital letter of a word (all German nouns are capitalized), Rilke meant the beginning or possibility of whatever the word signified.[36] Thus the acrobats represent the possibility of enduring life patiently, of persevering and striving in spite of the sorrows and limitations which they experience. It is significant that Rilke used "Dastehen," to stand there, rather than "Dasein," to be there, which emphasizes the physical aspect of the role of the acrobats, for they, like all mankind, are physical entities placed within a world of physical reality where they are buffeted about relentlessly. Their lot as playthings of life is compared to that of the pewter plates which King Augustus the Strong of Saxony (1670–1733), later King of Poland, sometimes rolled up to entertain his guests.[37]

18    The next section presents the acrobatic performance as a whole in the symbol of a rose. The spectators come and stand like petals around the performers, who are like the pistil of the rose which the pollen—the dust—

21  fertilizes. "The pounder"—"der Stampfer"—is one who stamps his foot, perhaps the lead acrobat who signals the beginning of the acrobatic act in this manner and sets the timing, but it may also be a ram, a pestle, or a pounder with technological connotations as in "die stampfende Maschine." "Der Stempel" is not only the botanical term, pistil, but also refers to the piston in a machine, so that the two terms may imply a view of modern man reduced to the level of a machine in the repetitive, empty performance of the acrobatic routine. The terms, "Stampfer" and "Stempel" also conjure up phallic images related to the rhythm of life as well as the rhythm of the

[36]Guardini, pp. 190–91.
[37]Steiner, p. 107.

performance, giving three distinct layers of meaning in these two terms related in both sound and meaning. The critics in general are uncertain whether "der Stampfer" refers to an individual acrobat or to the acrobats as a group. The singular form of the noun seems to indicate an individual, but the complete picture of the acrobats surrounded by the crowd of on-lookers would indicate the entire troupe as the pistil in the center of the rose. Unlike the rose, the fruit which the acrobats produce is false; it is the mere semblance of perfection. Like their audience, they themselves remain unaware of the futility of their endeavor, for they hide it under the glittering, shallow surface of show business glamor and the fixed smile of the performer. The smile of the audience is as superficial as that of the performers, for the performance merely entertains and distracts them. They find no deep or lasting meaning in it. Yet later the smile is seen to have positive value, for it denotes a willing acceptance of the burden of life wherein lies the significance of these acrobats.

From the general picture of the acrobatic performance we turn to an examination of the individual members of the troupe. The first one examined is the former weight-lifter now grown old who has shrunk up so that his skin appears large enough for two men. Now he only beats the drum for the performance, recalling certain traits in the figure of Père Rollin in the letter of 14 July 1907.

The young man is described in German quite literally as the son of a neck and a nun, where neck implies a muscular man. The meaning of the combination is shown in the second half of the description: he combines muscle or physical perfection with the innocence, the guilelessness, of a nun.[38] His innocence, however, derives from ignorance and inexperience, not from the innate harmony of children and animals.

The next four lines return to the function of the entire troupe in the elegy. Pointing ahead to the role of sorrow in the tenth elegy, the acrobats are described as toys given to a child sorrow. As playthings of the capriciousness of a child, these acrobats know sorrow; they are exposed to the heartbreaks of life without defense. But although they endure their sorrow patiently, they remain unaware of its positive role; they are the toys of external forces and lack inner stability.

From this interlude highlighting the positive possibility of sorrow and

[38]Steiner, p. 110.

suffering in human life, the elegy describes the figures of the children and their deeper reality. The first figure is that of the boy whose description returns to the fruit symbolism. The acrobatic act of which he is part has not yet reached perfection, and the child who is supposed to balance on the others is not yet able to do so. In terms of the seasons the act does not reach the maturity of autumn. Like unripe fruit in summer, the young boy falls prematurely over and over again as the acrobats continually practice. He falls against the earth which is the ultimate grave of everyone, emphasizing the double image of the danger of the acrobatic activity and the finiteness of all human life.[39] From this picture we turn to one of the positive possi-

46    bilities of the child—his love for his mother which the harshness of such life has not yet destroyed. He tries to express his love in a tender look, to break through the crust of physical existence and express his inner nature, but his human emotion is destroyed in the world of cruel reality. He is unable to communicate his love to his mother, for her tenderness has been destroyed by the harshness of her life.[40] Almost immediately the child is called back to the unceasing practice that is his life and the pain of the leaps and falls which his smile surmounts.

58    The following section of four lines, like the four-line unit preceding the one devoted to the boy, is a brief interlude highlighting the meaning of the acrobats and signifying a transition from a negative to a positive view of life. The positive aspect is emphasized by the presence of the angel who comes to collect the acrobat's smile and store it under its Latin name, "Subrisio Saltat." Since the smile is only human, it is limited or small-flowered; yet it represents the presence of the absolute world in man's inner

60    being, lending meaning and therefore joy to life in spite of its tribulations. It is to be praised as a healing herb, even though we do not entirely comprehend its meaning, for it belongs to the joys of the angel world beyond our comprehension.

62    From this interlude we turn to the figure of the little girl denied her childhood and imprisoned within the silk and fringes of her costume. Deprived of the freedom to be a child, she is offered for sale in the marketplace like fruit on the pans of a scale. In the second section the fruit of the rose symbol was false, the young boy falling was described as unripe fruit,

---

[39]Guardini, p. 200.
[40]Guardini, p. 201.

and here the girl is described as fruit of equanimity, stressing her reduction to the status of an unfeeling thing. Fruit and fruitfulness generally have a positive connotation for Rilke, but the fruit of the acrobats is human and therefore faulty. The last phrase of this section which has been translated "in the midst of shoulders" could also be translated "below the shoulders" since the German "unter" means both "among" and "under." The critics disagree about the meaning, and it is possible that Rilke meant to imply both meanings. It may portray the child being held up before the audience, but this phrase may also highlight the physical nature of what is for sale—the human body or physique in contrast to mind or soul. Additional insight into the symbolism may be provided from the field of sculpture since Rilke's long concern with the plastic arts is well known. A bust commonly portrays the subject from the shoulders up, and this portion of the human body represents the unique qualities of the individual—the qualities of mind and soul which are not for sale.[41] The picture as a whole is clear. What can be more pitiful than for a child to be denied the opportunity to be a child, to be deprived of one of the truly great positive areas of human life? Yet that is the lot of these children and still they smile and accept it.

The next section turns from examination of the individual acrobats to study the nature of their action. After long practice before achieving perfection, the act suddenly falls into place, and everything comes off with the smoothness of perfect coordination. Since the constant effort of the acrobats produces only physical perfection which becomes empty routine after it has been achieved, their success remains an illusion. The last two lines of this section summarize the significance of the acrobats for the elegies and provide a transition to the following section. "Die vielstellige Rechnung" could be a "many-digited number" as others have translated it, but it could also be a long sum or a complex equation. It clearly stands for the complexities of life in the bounded world of physical reality. "Zahlenlos aufgeht" could indicate that the number or equation equals zero, as some critics think, or it could also mean that the equation balances or that it equals infinity or boundlessness. The resolution of the mathematical expression can thus stand for death as the ultimate limitation (equals zero); for death as the other side of life, as a transformation into the boundless world of the

---

[41] This suggestion was made to me by Professor Harvey I. Dunkle, a colleague at San Diego State University.

hereafter (equals infinity); or for the coordination of the worlds of man and angel (balances). Furthermore, the boundless world appears within the real world in man's inner realm, so that this figure could encompass the coordinate existence of the worlds of man and the angel, of the here and the hereafter, and the simultaneous existence of bounded reality and the unbounded inner realm within man's world. Since the fifth elegy is structurally the center of the elegies, it is the balance point between these two worlds. The acrobats balance the positive and negative aspects of life against each other, which is their significance for the elegies.

*87*     In the next-to-last section the stage of the acrobats suddenly becomes the stage of life. As the figure of an unknown will propels the acrobats about, the figure of Madame Lamort—death—propels mankind. Madame Lamort is not organic death developing within the individual as a part of life; she is the death which is imposed from without, murdering life. Her death is capricious because it is external and therefore beyond control. It is like a public performance because its essential ingredient is appearance. With its cheap, artificial decorations, it is a fitting end—a winter hat where winter is equated with death[42]—to a life of destiny. Destiny here connotes all the conflicting and confusing bonds and ties which come from without, a life at the mercy of external forces and lacking inner stability like that of the acrobats.

*89*     The final section transposes the perfection of the acrobats on the physical plane to the perfection of love in the angel world. Love is related to the angel world when it is an inner absolute no longer linked to a specific object. Since man can never fully know the angel world in life, this section is in the subjunctive, emphasizing the unattainability of this level for the living. Although love belongs to both worlds, as an absolute it can reach perfection only when freed into the infinity of the angel. There in the perfection of complete transformation lovers may be able to execute acts of love as the
*105*     acrobats perform their acts on the physical plane. The smile of the acrobats then would become the true smile of the lovers,[43] and their carpet would be stilled. The search for perfection would be over, and their wanderings would end in attainment of joys not yet revealed to the living. Life with all its limitations offers man the possibility of patient endurance, willing

[42]Guardini, p. 217.
[43]Guardini, p. 224.

acceptance of the challenge of life, and the possibility of love. But perfection beyond the physical level lies outside the experience of the living. Genuinely absolute love is the ultimate reality which in the limited reality of human life the lover can reach only in momentary self-transcendence. The rows of onlookers surrounding the acrobats become the audience of dead who applaud and reward the lovers, denoting the significance of love in the absolute world of the hereafter.

The fifth elegy stands in the middle of the cycle as the balance point between the positive and negative aspects of human life. On the one side are the negative elements of the innate limitations of physical reality which buffet man about and the ultimate limitations of death and man's awareness of it. The fulcrum, the transition from the negative to the positive, is located almost exactly half way through the elegies where the approving angel appears to accept the smile of the acrobat.[44] On the other side of the balance are the positive elements of love, patient endurance, and acceptance of sorrow as a meaningful element inherent in our existence as physical entities. Although the world of the angel remains separated from our physical world, there are signs pointing to its coordination with ours. Wherever such signs may be found in the elegies, they are signified by the appearance of the angel and lend greater depth and increased meaningfulness to our own world of physical reality.

[44]Stahl, p. xvi.

The sixth elegy was begun in 1912, but most of the final version was written in 1913. The first thirty-one lines including the fig tree section were written in January and February 1913 in Ronda in Spain and the last three lines in late autumn 1913 in Paris. The remaining section expanding the Samson theme was added in 1922. Structurally the sixth elegy is the first of a group of elegies presenting the positive aspects of life. It counterbalances the fourth elegy with its emphasis on man's view of life as a duality. In the sixth elegy the symbols for Being as a unity wherein life and death become obverse sides of the same totality appear one after the other. Common to all of these symbols is the absence of growth and development.

1    The first symbol for nearly instantaneous fruitfulness is the fig tree. The blossoms of the fig tree are clustered within an outer sac which has the form of the fruit rather than the blossom. Insects must enter this covering through a small opening in the end in order to fertilize the blossoms so that the process of fertilization is inner or secret. The fig tree thus appears to spring directly into fruitfulness without the intermediate flowering stage.[45] In this elegy fruitfulness implies the development of a full life productive of meaningfulness and also the presence of the fruit of death as an organic part of life itself. When the goal of life is fruitfulness, action—life—and goal—death—are identical, and life and death become an inseparable unity. The

5    branches of the fig tree, which grow downward before turning upward at the tip, are compared to a fountain where the hydrostatic pressure causing the water to rise is created by introducing the water into the fountain at a height as far below the level of the fountain as the jet of water is to rise.[46] Thus the two configurations—the image of the sap of the tree and the water jet of the fountain—gather energy through an initial downward flow for a final leap into fruitfulness. The image of instant fruitfulness is repeated in the sudden transformation of Zeus into a swan in the legend of Leda resulting in the immediate fulfillment of his desires.

8    For ordinary mortals, however, the beginning and the end appear to be separated by a long development. They prize the flowering stage—their youthfulness—and wish to remain in the springtime of life rather than to recognize that all the seasons of life have value. Such people, like the

[45]Kreutz, p. 92.
[46]Steiner, p. 130.

acrobats in the fifth elegy, are controlled by external circumstances. Their lives are dominated by distractions and confusion and find no unity of purpose and meaningfulness. By lingering in the blossom, they retard the development of the fruit of death as a part of life; when death comes, it is imposed from without like the death of Madame Lamort.

15    One image for the view of life and death as a unity has already appeared in the elegies in those who die young. Like the animals, the child lives in harmony with his world; he has not become aware of its existence as something outside himself, is not separated from it as subject. Being unaware of death as end, he accepts it as part of life. The sixth elegy adds another exception to the usual view of life as a polarity where life is viewed as a rising curve and the end as a falling curve. In the hero's life death is organically integrated by the husbandman death—in contrast to the common image of the grim reaper—who cultivates his fruit within men. The falling and then rising configuration of the fig tree and the fountain of the first part of this elegy corresponds to the pattern in the life of the hero. Death bends the veins of the hero and of those who die young differently— like the fig tree and the fountain. For them death is seen as a rising curve since it is a continuation of life itself.

7    The smile of the acrobats signified acceptance of life in spite of its limitations. But for the hero and those destined to die young the limitations, especially the ultimate one of death, are sublimated into totality and are no longer experienced as boundaries. Thus they precede their smile, for they represent a more harmonious stage of development than the acrobats. The comparison to Egyptian sculpture points ahead to the landscape of the tenth elegy.

0    Rilke's hero is not characterized by specific goals in life, for the very nature of life itself would cause such goals to change continually. The hero of the elegies is an existential hero whose actions are determined by deep inner necessity—the kind of person he is—rather than by external purposes and goals. His goals and actions are identical so that his life is a unity from beginning to end; he *is*, he does not grow or develop. His ability to choose and to make himself lies even before his beginning; when the choice is made, it applies to his entire life. Unlike ordinary mortals who seek permanence, he recognizes change as the very basis of life, with insecurity and danger inherent in it. Thus "he is forever moving onward into the changed constellation of his continual danger" where those who seek permanence and security cannot follow. Since his affirmation and accep-

tance of change as the very basis of life is in accord with the nature of the dynamic universe, this pattern is exalted for its harmony and placed among the stars shining in both the human and the angel worlds while the false pattern of duality receives no affirmation.

29    The following section of four lines repeats the exaltation of the pattern of the hero with the subjunctive wish to be young again and able to follow the example of the Biblical hero, Samson. The subjunctive form emphasizes the unattainability of the hero's life for all but a few rare exceptions. Although man may recognize validity in such a life, it remains beyond his reach.

32    The nature of the hero's life determines the nature of his relationship to woman both as mother and loved one. His love like that of the child in the fourth elegy is an inner absolute, not love for an external object or goal. As in the fourth elegy, the immanent reality of the loved one is transformed into absolute reality, transcending the object in the transformation. On the positive side, such love is indestructable; but on the negative side lies the tragedy of growing beyond those one loves. Since the hero cannot allow his love to bind him to another, for this would deflect his unity of purpose,

40    he brings sorrow to those he loves when he outdistances them. The ravines into which maidens plunge are related to the ravines of the third elegy so that the sexual aspect of love symbolized in the primeval forest bears suffering and sorrow for the woman as well as for the man. The sexual act of love divides the unified world of the child from the fragmented adult world with the result that such experience represents a plunge into the chaos resulting from irreversible severance of childhood unity into seg-

43    ments. The hero's love, like that of the child, is characterized by unity; it is free, not bound to an object. He surmounts the experience of love rather than allowing it to draw him into the world of ties and bonds to others.

Rilke's hero acts from a deep inner unity where goals are identical with the course of his life. Exterior goals do not exist for him, for they would lie outside his already determined basic course. Identity of goal and action is a concept which appears in Zen Buddhism, a philosophy in which Rilke shared an interest with his philosopher friend, Rudolf Kassner.[47] The hero,

---

[47]Rudolf Kassner, "Rainer Maria Rilke—wie ich ihn sah," *Die Zeit* (27 December 1956), p. 6. Rilke might also have become acquainted with this concept through the study of Aristotle's *Nichomachean Ethics*, where Aristotle says that the highest activity is that activity whose goal is intrinsic to itself.

like the child—including those destined to die young—and the animals, lives in oneness with the universe so that death and life are integral parts of a whole where death appears as a continuation of life and a rising curve. In recognizing and seeking change as the very basis of life, the hero paradoxically attains enduring unity. The hero thus functions as a symbol for life and death as a unity in contrast to the duality which dominated the fourth elegy.

The seventh elegy was written in Muzot on 7 February 1922, the final version of the conclusion on 26 February 1922. Structurally it continues the basic and significant positive turn which began with the sixth elegy, presenting the positive aspects of love in contrast to the negative, erotic side of love in the third one. Love provides man with a unique mode of relationship to the angel, for in love man creates things which combine existence and essence. When he takes such objects into his inner world, he shows them to the angel who cannot perceive them as reality. Love is thus man's window to transcendence, and it becomes neither necessary nor desirable to draw the angel into the human world.

The very beginning of the poem provides a clue to the new orientation when man's attempt to woo the angel, to summon the angel into the earthly sphere, is rejected as outgrown. The hiatus between man and the angel was delineated in the first elegy where the experience was so painful that it produced the desperate cry of the opening lines which despaired of finding meaning within the human sphere alone. The seventh elegy repeats the theme of separation between the world of man and that of the angels, but here it is accepted as the established order. The affirmation of the disjunctive nature of the two spheres is so strong that the earlier longing of man for the angel and his desire to bring the angel realm into his own world is rejected not only as impossible but also undesirable.

1    The first section compares man's wooing of the angel to two images— the song of the bird in the springtime and the wooing of lovers. We have already noted that the bird is related to the angel both as winged creature and through its oneness with the universe. Lovers, too, are related to the angel world, for beyond the reality of specific love there opens up the absolute value of the act of love, enabling the individual to transcend momentarily his limited reality and to sense the absolute world of the angel. Yet even these figures of the bird and the lovers which stand at the outermost limits of life touching the angel realm beyond are living creatures subject to all the innate limitations of physical reality. They are earthbound and therefore unable to communicate with the angel as absolute to absolute, and the angel as absolute has no place in their world. Man must therefore renounce his longing for that which he cannot know and cease trying to pull down into his sphere that which does not belong there. He must forsake

wooing the angel, even though he could woo as ethereally as the song of the lark in spring or as intensely as the wooing of lovers. He must find his meaning within his own world.

10   The second section reiterates the image of the song of the lark in spring, rising from the first tentative chirps to the final soaring trill. But like the
15   rising jet of a fountain, the flight of the bird and the swelling song are not rising curves alone. Predictably they contain within themselves a falling curve as well; the rise of the water jet and the flight of the bird are still subject to the force of gravity, and the flight of the bird and its song are limited by its mortality. Yet precisely here the change in mood from the previous elegies becomes perfectly clear. In the earlier elegies the theme of man's limitations would have signified a downward pessimistic turn; here it causes no more than a slight hesitation, a momentary pause, before the song of praise continues for the birds, the trees, the flowers and all the marvels and beauties of nature flourishing in the benign warmth of summer. The rising song of praise for all nature including human life parallels the swelling song of the lark in the first portion of this section and culminates in the themes of sleep and night with their mythological evocation of death. But now the theme of death does not bring even momentary hesitation. The rising curve of praise continues and we pass almost imperceptibly from the human to the angel world, prefiguring the path of the youth in the
7   tenth elegy. The linking element here as there is the stars which are common to both worlds. They are the manifestations of the absolute realm visible in man's world, although only imperfectly, as the real stars are only imperfectly visible, the light rays distorted by the atmosphere through which they must pass. Only in death can man know them perfectly, whereby even the ultimate limitation of death becomes a rising instead of a falling curve as it is in the sixth elegy for those destined to die young and for the hero. The coexistence of the two worlds suffices to lend value to human life. The urge to bring the angel into our world is no longer needed or wanted. Our world has value, too, as this song of praise attests.

)   The following section returns to the theme of the final lines of the first one, the wooing of lovers. The love which calls is the love of Gaspara Stampa in the first elegy, the universal love of the child in the fourth elegy, and the love of the hero in the closing lines of the sixth elegy. The call of such love is not possessively directed toward a single object; it has become a timeless absolute which penetrates beyond the human world to the realm

103

of the dead where maidens respond. All who are in the realm of the dead could perceive such a call, but only those whose lives had been deficient on earth would wish to desert the perfection of the realm of the dead for the limitations of human life. Those who come are mistakenly answering the call of eroticism described in the third elegy. They are like Christine Brahe in *Malte Laurids Brigge* who remains in this world as a ghost, unable to find in death the angel world which she had never known in life, or like the earlier mothers in the river bed of inheritance in the third elegy.[48] The caller gently explains to them the nature of their error: they have failed to seek the quality of intensity in life.[49] Only in moments of greatest intensity can an understanding be reached which transcends the level of factual knowledge to find a unity of man's inner and outer worlds which beyond childhood is his sole contact in life with the angel realm. Such a moment of intensity lends value to all of human life, and it is a function of quality rather than quantity.[50] Love is a primary path to this experience, for true love more than any other emotion is characterized by intensity.[51] In love for an individual, the lover in the depth of his feeling may transcend the

*38* limiting effect of the object to find pure love itself and thus in the blissful chase pass beyond the loved one into the absolute world of universal love, of nothingness and limitless space. This nothingness is not the obverse of something or physical reality but of the bounded world of subject-object vision; it is boundlessness. In such love the lover once again may find temporarily the same oneness and harmony with the universe which was the child's way of life.

*39* In the next section Rilke restates once more his emphatic affirmation of the value of human life. Yet many would ask how all human life could be meaningful. What meaning could possibly be found in the lives of those like the acrobats of the fifth elegy? Where is there meaning or value in the lives of the poor in the ghettos and slums of the cities where life is made of frustration, desperation, and privation? Yet these seemingly deprived ones experience moments of intensity which make even lives such as theirs meaningful. The true value of human life is the inner, intangible realm of intensity where in momentary self-transcendence the individual senses a

[48]Guardini, p. 265.
[49]Kreutz, p. 105.
[50]Guardini, p. 266.
[51]Buddenberg, pp. 194–95.

harmonious universe wherein he himself plays a meaningful role. Significantly it is again maidens who even in these circumstances achieve validity, for the third elegy has already pointed to Rilke's belief that woman is freer than man and thus more capable of rising above the specific to the universal. The really deprived ones of our world are not those who live in material want, but those who are poor in spirit. They search for value in the world of possessions, success, and good fortune with its rewards of recognition and the envy of others. Their laughter is superficial and disharmonious like the false goals of happiness and prosperity which they seek. It bears no relation to the smile of the fifth elegy. They never learn that they are pursuing a chimera, that in grasping for the fleeting external world, they have missed the permanence and value of the inner world. They are truly poor, for the real riches of human life lie beyond their reach in the intangible, inner realm.

The following section continues the theme of the inner world, the structure of which is expanded and elucidated. In addition to the duality of inner and outer spheres, the one usually considered the inner sphere is also a duality. One part of it is the mind. and the mind relates to the factual external world. The pictures in the following lines describe what modern industry calls rationalization of production where the world is treated solely as a physical phenomenon. It constructs buildings and houses to serve specific purposes, and the deeper intangible attributes of love, feeling, and beauty fall away, for they are not functions of the mind.[52] The external world which was once enriched with meaning has been stripped of all except practical function; it has shrunk into less and less.[53] The ultimate product of our age is the power plant. Although the power it produces is intangible, it is of momentary duration, a suitable symbol for the fleeting impermanence of all life and the physical backdrop before which it plays. Such power is without form and meaning, of value only for what it produces. The reference to tense energy may imply beyond the specific energy form all the aimless busyness and rush of modern life. Many Rilke scholars criticize Rilke for an inability to relate to the modern industrial world. Yet here he has comprehended and described one of the chief difficulties facing modern industry: the lowering of productivity due to the inability of workers to relate to work whose meaning is derived solely from

[52]Kreutz, p. 108.
[53]Guardini, p. 272.

income earned by it. Extensive studies have shown that modern job satisfaction is derived more from a feeling of accomplishing something meaningful and from a sense of being valued for this accomplishment than from salary.[54]

The world has not always been so limited. Once man related to his world differently. Beyond the involvement of his mind was the additional involvement of the second element of the inner world which Rilke calls "heart." This is closely related to Karl Jaspers's concept of "soul," that part of man which stands in relationship to God, or in Rilkean terminology, the absolute world of the angel. Here Rilke introduces in the elegies his second path of man's relationship to the angel, the inner path which is uniquely human.[55] The temples of this stanza are any structure which was created with love and deep concern and has been loved and venerated. They exist not only as visible, tangible, real entities but also invisibly within the

60   hearts of those who love them. In this way they bridge the worlds of man and the angel. But modern man who judges everything in terms of practical use, who either denies or disregards the existence of the world of the heart, ignores or fails to appreciate such structures. He sees them only as physical entities and does not recreate them within his heart where they might acquire the true permanence of the absolute.

63   We live in a time of transition. The past and its temples no longer have meaning for us; our age has been disinherited. We have lost our sense of direction and cannot relate to the future. The inability to relate to the future can become positive if it strengthens our ties to the past and directs our attention to preserving in both the inner and outer worlds those structures of the past which stand as monuments to the unity of the temporal and the

67   eternal. Like all constructions of man, such structures exist in the temporal world and are as subject as any modern cerebral creation to change and destruction. Yet in all their impermanence they stand as witnesses to the presence of the absolute world of the stars within our own, drawing the stars from their eternal, unchanging realm into ours. All such structures are temples whether they serve a religious function or not, for they are of the angel world. As such they can be shown to the angel, who can see only what

---

[54]Frederick Herzberg, *Work and the Nature of Man* (Cleveland and New York: The World Publishing Co., 1966), pp. 72–73.

[55]Guardini, p. 316.

is absolute and for whom all that was created without love remains invisible.[56] Examples of such structures are pillars which reach for the heavens, pylons which form the entrances to Egyptian tombs and symbolize man's ability to enter the absolute world, the sphinx which towers with its human face to the stars, and cathedral spires soaring in their upward thrust above the changing world of man. All these examples illustrate man's upward reach toward the angel world. Towers and pylons may also be regarded as phallic symbols,[57] reiterating the role of love as window to the absolute. This oneness of human and angel worlds which can be attained even within our own limited reality may be the basis for the dedication of the next elegy to Rudolf Kassner, who relates it to the Buddhist concept of "Zen," which he believes to be characteristic of his own and Rilke's works. He describes it as unity of thought and action, of goal and striving for the goal, of having no concept or theory to separate goal and action which are thus sublimated into a unity of Being.[58]

Man's imprisonment in the world of time and space has aspects of limitation, yet using this space is also man's unique opportunity. Miraculously he can unite in what he creates in his own earthly space the realms of heaven and earth, of man and the angel. Such an accomplishment deserves man's highest praise, which is the function of this elegy, but since such creation also extends into the angel realm, all that man creates with love is worthy of the praise of the angel as well. Even the angel must acknowledge such accomplishments as Chartres; or music, which lacking in external form can soar even higher as pure configuration of emotion;[59] or greatest of all, the experience of love which in transcending its object reaches the angel realm. They are expressions of the absolute within our own world.

The final section returns to the opening theme. Man should not try to summon the angel into his earthly sphere. The realms of man and the angel are forever separated;[60] the absolute world of the angel could only be terrible to man. This does not mean that man cannot stand in relationship to the angel, but that rather than seeking the absolute directly, he must seek

---

[56]Rilke, *Briefe* II, 485.

[57]Marcel Kunz, *Narziss. Untersuchungen zum Werk Rainer Maria Rilkes* (Bonn: Bouvier, 1970), p. 77.

[58]Kassner, p. 6.

[59]Steiner, p. 178.

[60]Guardini, p. 288.

it within his own finite world of time and space where, in all that he creates with love, infinity is also expressed. Man's call to the angel is therefore like an outstretched arm reaching upward in search for absolute values, but the hand remains open as defense against angel awesomeness and as admonition to the angel to remain within his own realm. Man's hand could grasp only what is object for him. The absolute angel cannot become object for man, for it can enter only man's inner world, not the outer object world of reality. Thus the problem stated in the first elegy of the relationship between man and the angel reaches its solution in the seventh elegy. Although the realms of man and angel are forever separated, man can find the absolute within his own world in love and in utilizing his space for objects which he creates with love and transforms into enduring inner absolute being related to the angel world. From the final resolution of the problems of the relationship between man and angel stated with such anguish in the first elegy now springs in the second section of the seventh elegy a lyrical song in praise of life scarcely surpassed anywhere and a decisive turn toward complete acceptance and praise of human life including all its limitations.

# THE EIGHTH ELEGY

The eighth elegy was written on 7 and 8 February 1922 and is dedicated to Rudolph Kassner, an Austrian poet and philosopher whose friendship with Rilke began in 1907.[61] Rilke and Kassner were interested in similar philosophical problems, which accounts for the dedication of this elegy.

In the seventh elegy man's sphere of activity and his meaning were found to lie in his world of physical reality, and the eighth elegy delineates man's relationship to that sphere. Information is sought in the animal's relationship to the universe and what this reveals by contrast about man's dissimilar mode of life. A significant aspect of this problem is man's subject-object division, which is usually experienced as an absolute barrier and which is present as long as man's attention is directed toward the external world. Beginning with the first elegy, Rilke's universe has been divided into the major fragments of the human world and the angel world. If the elegies are arranged around the fifth one as an axis, the eighth corresponds to the second. The second one elaborates the first major division of the universe as man sees it into absolute and physical reality, while the eighth continues the process of fracture into the world of physical reality so that in being separated from the remaining world of living creatures, man becomes a unique entity.[62] Immediately there arises the question of what Rilke classifies as creature or animal. A letter to Lou Andreas-Salomé written 20 February 1914 is devoted to this theme and provides important information for this and other aspects of the elegies:

> I have conceived of it beautifully, as I never imagined it before: transposition of the developing creature from the world further and further into the inner realm. Therefore the charming state of the bird on its way inward; its nest is after all almost an external womb provided for it by nature which it merely equips and covers over, instead of receiving it complete. So it is that one of the animals which has a very special sense of trust toward its external world, as if it knew that it shared a very deep secret with it. Therefore it sings in it as if it were singing in its inner being: therefore we take the sound of a bird so easily into our

[61] Steiner, p. 185.

[62] Karl-Heinz Fingerhut, *Das Kreatürliche im Werke Rainer Maria Rilkes* (Bonn: Bouvier, 1970). This work gives a very extensive treatment of this theme consonant with my ideas on the subject.

being: it seems to us as if we transform it completely in our emotion; indeed, for a moment it can transform the entire world into inner space for us because we sense that the bird does not distinguish between its heart and that [of the world]. On the one hand now much is gained for the animal and human spheres by transposition of maturing life into a womb: for it becomes all the more world when externally the participation of the world in these processes is reduced (as if it had become more unsure, as if it had been taken away—), on the other hand (from my notebook, written last year in Spain—you will remember the question): "What is the source of the intimacy of the creature (of the others)? [It comes] from maturing outside the body, which means that it never leaves the sheltering body. (All its life is like a fetus.) . . . ."

That which the plant shows so beautifully, the way it makes no secret of its secret as if having knowledge that it could not be otherwise than in security: it is exactly that, just imagine, which I experienced in Egypt before the sculptures and since then always experienced with things from Egypt: this baring of the secret which is so through and through, so all over secret that it does not need to be hidden. And perhaps everything phallic (as I sensed in the Temple of Karnak, for I still could not think it) is only a revelation of the human secretively secret in the sense of the openly secret in nature. I can never think of the smile of the Egyptian gods without the word "flower pollen" occurring to me.[63]

The creature world is separated on the one side from the world of man by subject-object division and on the other side from the world of things by the element of life. This segment of the universe covers a wide range from the flower which exists in pure harmony with nature, through the insects which being born directly into the world live their entire lives as if in a protective womb, the birds which combine the protective security of the womb (nest) with the ultimate insecurity of flight, the animal which senses its physical existence and by contrast a prior greater harmony, and finally the child. Although the range of living things within these borders is great, they are unified by their mode of existence in direct harmony with the universe, by their feeling of oneness with it in contrast to man's separation from it by the self-awareness of the subject-object relationship. Yet man himself is not born with this self-awareness, so that as a child he, too, belongs to this creature world, as Rilke's reference to the "other" creatures in the

---

[63]Rilke, *Briefe*, I, 489–90. [My own translation.]

letter to Lou Andreas-Salomé indicates. Since the opening lines state that the animal or creature "sees" openness, the question arises concerning the inclusion of the flower in the creature world. It does not have eyes as the animals do, yet poetically both English and German speak of flowers seeing and having eyes. It is important to remember that here we are not dealing with scientific classification but with a poetic symbol. The proximity of the flower to the creature world in both the letter just quoted and in the eighth elegy with similar symbolism in both provides some justification for including it in Rilke's creature world.

A second major problem of definition occurs within the first sentence: openness. Openness is not to be equated with the absolute or angel world; it is instead the creature's view of the universe which is the opposite of man's object vision. In the letter to Hulewicz, Rilke speaks of a universe where there is no here and no hereafter, but only a great unity in which the angel is at home.[64] Death is the element which divides our universe into a here and a hereafter; our foreknowledge of it separates us from the remainder of the creature world, limits our vision, and breaks our world into fragments. Since the animal or creature does not perceive the demarcation of death, it sees the world as a unity including both the world of man and that of the angel. It is a part of its world, not separated from it as subject from object.[65] Openness thus is an unbounded view where life and death are parts of the same unity,[66] where life is not bounded by death nor observation by subject-object barriers.

The vision which is the theme of the eighth elegy is essentially philosophical rather than physical, although Steiner demonstrates interesting correspondences between the physical and philosophical aspects.[67] He says the animal does not see perspectively, which means that the animal does not order or arrange what it sees with reference to itself so that it does not sense a separation from its world. In contrast, man with his sense of perspective and self-awareness sees his world in relationship to himself. As the only living being with self-awareness, he is also conscious of his inability to escape from his imprisonment within his physical existence; he alone recognizes the limiting, fracturing effect of physical reality. In not imposing

[64]Rilke, *Briefe*, II, 480–81. [My own translation.]
[65]Steiner, p. 198.
[66]Guardini, pp. 292–93.
[67]Steiner, pp. 186–87.

a false order on what it sees, the animal beholds unbounded openness. But when man sees the animal, he sees it in relation to himself, fitting it into the world which he organizes from his perspective in its center as experiencing subject.

Since man exists in both time and space, his perception has implications for time as well as space. Man commonly perceives time as a continuum of past, present, and future. From the perspective of the present moment to which his physical existence limits him, he sees only the past; the future he can merely surmise. His vision is therefore reversed, turned to the past and spatially bounded. He looks back to the past, whereas the animal looks forward into an unbounded world.[68] When he sees the animal, he adapts it to his own world of time and space, trapping it there and limiting or hindering its freedom. Yet from the countenance of the animal which seems not to see our world, we can infer the existence of a unified, harmonious totality completely different from our own world view. Countenance

5  is used to translate the German "Antlitz," which Rilke uses differently from "Gesicht," face. "Antlitz" or countenance signifies unity of inner and outer worlds, while "Gesicht" or face stands for the external world of reality as in the outside face of the doll in the fourth elegy. Only at the beginning and the end of life does man escape his view of life as segmented. The child, not being born with an awareness of death, sees the world initially as the animals do and thus belongs to the creature world. But experience, example, and normal development soon transform his mode of vision into the subject-object relationship of the adult world with its awareness of death cutting off the view of what lies beyond. Being unaware of death the animal looks

12  not backward to the past as man does, but forward into an undivided totality where God or the angel exists. For this reason it goes not to death as man does, but to eternity wherein it merely undergoes transformation within the totality. The conclusion of this section compares the creature world to the fountain. For Rilke flowing water symbolizes the paradox of that which remains forever the same while continually changing, the paradox of man and angel, time and eternity, of change and permanence.

13  The creature world, like the fountain, is a paradoxical unity of physical reality and the angel absolute since the reality of the creature is unbounded like that of the angel. Beyond man's imprisonment within physical reality

[68]Steiner, p. 199.

he senses the existence of a comprehensive unity—pure space—which animals and the child experience directly.

14     The second section continues the contrast between the creature world of flowers, animals, and children, and our human world. The space of the creature world is pure and unconstrained, a nowhere without a negative. As nowhere it is unbounded, lacking the ultimate negation of death. The plant knows perfectly—for it knows no contrast—that it exists in complete security in a universe where nothing is lost but only undergoes transformation. Knowing perfectly, it accepts perfectly without any desires of its own to separate it from the universe with which it is in complete harmony. Sometimes the child knows this world, but those who cannot follow it there force it to return to their world of imposed order and purposefulness. At the other end of life those who come face to face with death no longer see it as demarcation and limit but see beyond to the absolute world of the angel, just as lovers in the act of perfect love transcend the object to reach beyond the human world to the inner absolute. But these moments of transcendence are transitory, and we are always recalled to our human world of finite reality which is our normal mode of existence and from which we can escape permanently only in death.

5     Since the animal's world view is so different from ours, it cannot communicate its message to us; it cannot change our pattern of life or restore us to primal unity.[69] Once again the contrast is stated: where our forward view is directed toward the future of continuous time with its final limit of death, the animal sees not time but eternity and pure, boundless space free from awareness of death.

3     The next section defines the place of the warm animal within the creature world, for even within the creature world there are degrees of security. The warm animal shares with man the memory of being more intimately one with the universe, more secure and protected in the womb, which makes its present abode less secure. Yet its mode of relation to life and to its world is still direct, unlike man, who only senses a unity from which he has become separated.

    From the warm animal Rilke turns to the opposite end of the animal spectrum to the tiny creature, the insect. Unlike the warm animal, it does not develop within a womb but is born directly into the world so that

---

[69]Buddeberg, p. 129.

having no memory of prior unity as the warm animal does, it experiences the world as womb. Since it never leaves the primal unity of the womb, it sees life within physical reality as the same unity with totality which it enjoyed before birth.

61     The bird bridges the world of the tiny creature and the warm animal. Like the insect it is born from eggs, but as the letter informed us, its nest is like a womb. Rilke compares this existence in both worlds to an Etruscan tomb with its sculpture of the dead on the cover. The dead figure within belongs to the angel world which man reaches perfectly in death, but the sculptured figure on the cover is man's concept of the individual as physical reality and belongs to the human world. Like the double figures of the Etruscan tomb, the bird is at home both on the earth and in the air, seeming in this way also to combine both worlds, for air bridges the space between world and heaven and is the portion of our world which is most non-physical—even though we know scientifically that it is as real as solid matter. The bird finds existence in both worlds perplexing, for although it can fly and sing as ethereally as the lark in spring in the seventh elegy, it is still a living creature. This perplexing combination of security and insecurity is captured in the picture of the darting flight of the bat flashing through the sky like a crack appearing in a cup, a crack of insecurity through the security of the womb.[70] The bat is less secure than the bird for it is not a bird, but a mammal, a warm-blooded animal; it is the creature that must fly, yet comes from a womb.

The end of the section returns to man, the spectator locked within himself and doomed to relate to everything as external object.[71] He relates to the object world by ordering and arranging it according to his own concepts from his subject perspective and for his use. But since he is an imperfect, limited creature, the world he makes is likewise imperfect and collapses, as he himself does in the end. Man has left the primal unity of the child behind, and his relation to the exterior world is determined by his imprisonment within time and space. He cannot overcome the subject–object barrier in an outward direction as the creature world does. Where the creature looks forward into boundless infinity, man looks backward at the finite past. As he

66     travels through life, he is like the traveler who, standing on a hill, looks

[70]Guardini, pp. 321–22.
[71]Guardini, pp. 322–23.

back for the last time at what he is leaving. Since man's view is bounded by finiteness and death, he alone of all creation is aware of always parting from what has been, of always losing what he has known, and so he lingers and looks back. This picture combines the past temporal aspect with space orientation backward in a symbol for human finiteness.

Man is set apart from the rest of physical reality, even from the warm-blooded animals most nearly like himself, by self-awareness with its subject-object barrier, by a prior knowledge of death which limits his view to his own world of physical reality, and by perspective vision which relates the world to the subject-observer. By isolating man from the creature world, the eighth elegy delineates man's unique position within the world, preparing for his unique function and value in the following elegy.

Rilke himself was unsure when the beginning of the ninth elegy (lines
1–6a) and lines 77–79 were written.[72] The *Complete Works* give the date of
March 1912 in Duino for these lines.[73] The remainder was written in
2   February 1922. The first lines contrast ordinary human life—destiny—with
the creature view of life in the symbol of the laurel leaf. As Steiner points
out, the symbolism of the laurel leaf is extraordinarily rich and complex.
In mythology the nymph Daphne, meaning laurel, the daughter of the
river god Peneus, was transformed into laurel when pursued by Apollo.
Apollo thereupon made himself a crown of laurel which was thereafter
associated with him. The sudden transformation from one mode of
existence to another parallels the sudden transformation of Zeus into a swan
in the legend of Leda in the sixth elegy, both of which symbolize a view of
death as transformation within a totality rather than as final end. The wave
shape of the edge of the leaf relates to water, symbolizing the paradoxical
unity of permanence and change. As the bird of the eighth elegy shows, the
contact edge of air and solid leaf represents the contact in man's heart of the
ethereal non-physical world and the world of physical reality within an
4   all-encompassing unity. As in the fifth elegy, the smile is an expression of
the absolute world of the angel within our human world and signifies
complete acceptance of the task of life. The laurel leaf is darker green than
other plants, connoting sorrow and death as the roots of life, while at the
same time it is an evergreen, demonstrating enduring life in its absence of
seasons.[74] As a part of the creature world, it summarizes all that the creature
world of the eighth elegy stands for: a view of life as harmonious existence
within a unity which is experienced spontaneously. Man's view of his
world as outside object, the significance of which lies in its usefulness for
him, results in a pragmatic evaluation of life and his surroundings. He seeks
security in possessions and ties to others and thereby desires destiny, for
possessions and ties are subject to all the impermanence of matter. Yet he
seeks to avoid acknowledgement of death as a part of life, so that he tries to
evade this portion of human destiny, revealing his lack of comprehension
of the nature and significance of life.

[72]Steiner, pp. 186–87.
[73]Rilke, *Sämtliche Werke*, I, 873.
[74]Steiner, pp. 208–11.

Structurally the ninth elegy corresponds to the first one, presenting the final development of the answers to the questions posed in the first elegy.

6    The second half of the first section gives us negative answers to the questions opening the ninth elegy, the inquiry for meaning and significance in the human sphere. Such meaning cannot be found in happiness, curiosity, or emotions. Happiness is temporary, a fleeting benefit, which attempts to deny man's roots in sorrow, suffering, and death. The search for happiness is an attempt to avoid recognizing and acknowledging man's limitations and impending death and can yield only negative results. Curiosity leads not to understanding of life or man's role in the universe, but to factual knowledge which relates to physical reality alone and is as lasting as the subjects which learn the knowledge and the objects with which it is concerned. Emotion is not totally negative, for it is an expression of the absolute in reality, but it could be expressed more perfectly in the spontaneous harmony of the laurel—the creature world—within the universe. For man even the most meaningful emotion of love is nearly always distorted by attachment to an object so that only in rare moments of transcendence can man even in this most intense feeling rise above his imprisonment in physical reality.

The second section turns to a positive answer to the question of meaning in human life. Like every living thing, the human being is finite; but unlike plants and animals, he is conscious of his finiteness through self-awareness. This awareness closes to him a direct relationship to totality of Being such as the animal enjoys, but it also opens to him a path within himself which is not open to plants and animals, for only man by virtue of his self-awareness can stand in relationship to himself.[75] Man is therefore unique, and this uniqueness imposes upon him a unique task: the duty of transformation. Man is the most fleeting of all living things, for he alone is aware of his finiteness,[76] yet in the physical world he can take impermanent reality into his inner realm where it is freed of the limitations of time and space and transformed into a non-physical absolute such as the angel knows perfectly. This is the only path between physical reality and the angel absolute, for although the creatures live in complete harmony with the universe, the sphere of reality is invisible to the angel. Only man can bridge this hiatus between actuality and the angel world so that the angel may see reality in its

[75]Guardini, p. 316.
[76]Guardini, p. 337.

transformed state in man's inner being as well as his own invisible absolute.[77] Because finite human life is unique in its nature and its task, it is valuable and should be accepted willingly and joyfully. The individual has no repetition; he lives just once. Therefore each has inherent value apart from his role as unit and link in the human race, and life has value beyond continuation of previous generations. This unique value of the individual does not enable man to transcend his limitations but to find meaning within his finite limits.[78]

The idea that man has a duty to establish a conscious relationship to his world also may be found in Fichte. Fichte points out that consciousness, including representation of physical objects, is the product of one ultimate cause in the universe, so that subject and object are related through their relation to this ultimate cause. The subject-object dichotomy causes man to experience objects only as manifestations of the thinking subject; yet as thinking subject, man can imagine no action of his own to be real without assuming something outside himself as object. This world of physical objects has no independent self-existence; it functions merely as the material for man's duty. Other ideas found in Rilke may also be found in Fichte. Fichte says that man cannot comprehend the infinite because man is finite. Man is a member of two orders, a spiritual one dominated by will and a sensuous one in which he operates by deed. His vocation—his function and his meaning—transcends time and space; to fulfill it he must raise his thoughts above sensory limitations. All of man's life is eternal because he is in the hand of the Creator, and no one can remove him from the Creator's hand. Man's mode of relationship to everything including the object world and the Creator is through thought; the animals in contrast relate spontaneously.

17 The third section inquires about the nature of man's unique responsibility. The first elegy has already stated that the world has need of us, and the seventh speaks both of making use of the space of physical reality which is man's unique sphere and of man's role as bridge between the existing reality of the creature world and the abstract perfection of the angel world.[79] Our area of responsibility thus lies within our own realm of physical reality

[77]Steiner, p. 213.
[78]Guardini, pp. 337–38.
[79]Buddeberg, pp. 281–82.

which we relate to the angel world through our unique inner being when we fulfill our responsibility and try to hold the whole world in our hearts, even though we cannot take this inner world with us when in death we enter the absolute realm of the hereafter.[80] Since we can show to the angel directly only that which belongs to the angel world, we can take with us to the hereafter only that which is absolute, only what is signified by the stars visible in both worlds: suffering, sorrow, and love—inexpressible concepts, which do not exist as the things do. It is better to leave these absolutes to the primordial perfection of the angel world, for to draw them into the human world, to "say" them even with intensity and love would be to give them finite reality, to bound what is essentially boundless. The stars—absolute values—are basically unsayable, for they are transcendent reality alone, whereas "to say" in the Rilkean sense represents a perfect combination of immanent and transcendent reality. Thus man can "say" only what exists in reality, not an abstract concept. This theme is portrayed in the imagery of the traveler to a rugged mountain slope. From the slope—the higher reality of sorrow, suffering, and love—the wanderer does not bring back what exists in abundance in the valley world of man—the soil of physical reality—but the gentian which flourishes only on the mountain slope, the word which grows in the soil of reality and unites the worlds of man and absolute as the two colors indicate. This word is not the ordinary word which only touches the surface of what it expresses; it unites actuality and essence to become one with the object.[81] All the examples of such words signify the unity of the worlds of man and of angel. House could stand for physical reality which is man's home and his unique opportunity and also for love which in its intensity bridges both worlds. Bridge accents man's role as intermediary between physical reality and the absolute through his unique inner reality. The flowing water of the fountain stands for the paradox of permanence and change, for a universe whose very permanence is derived dynamically from constant change, and the rising and then falling curve of the jet stands for life and death together. Gateway symbolizes man's ability to relate to both worlds and the inner sphere which is his mode of relationship. Jug relates to the potter by the Nile. It is made by hand with love, and as a laral object (laral in the sense of household deities) it enters our

---

[80]Steiner, p. 215.
[81]Guardini, p. 343.

inner world through love. When held under a stream of water, it is filled without hesitation, symbolizing the bounty of nature which in its innate creature harmony fulfills man's needs without question. Fruit tree refers to the sixth elegy where fruitfulness is praised in contrast to flowering and to the fruit of death which is within everyone and should ripen with growing understanding and acceptance so that life and death become a unity rather than mutually exclusive opposites. Window is the opening to the absolute provided by love and by man's unique inner world. Pillar and spire have appeared in the seventh elegy where they stand for man's upward reach for the absolute which he senses beyond his own realm. Man can fulfill his responsibility to the world of things expressed in these words when he transforms them by love into inner absolutes, a mode of relationship which external reality with its spontaneous existence cannot know or even dare to

*38*    imagine. Having different modes of life, man and nature do not communicate directly, yet the inherited urge to love is the threshold between man and nature, and between man's inner world and actuality.[82] In the self-transcendence of love man becomes completely open not only to the loved one but to everything around him,[83] enabling him to take the whole world into his heart. In the act of love the lovers transcend not only space but also time. As the third elegy pointed out, lovers are as physical entities links in the succeeding generations of the human race living in the time continuum of past, present, and future. Yet in the intensity of their emotion all time is concentrated in the present moment of love which becomes an existential absolute surviving unchanged in the inner world. Thus lovers transcend their role as links in the human race to accomplish with ease their responsibility to rescue ephemeral reality into non-corporeal existence within their inner world.[84]

*42*    In the seventh elegy man recognizes that the angel belongs in the primordial perfection of his own world, that man must renounce his desire to bring the angel into the world of actuality. Although man is the only link between the abstract angel realm and concrete reality, his home is the real world, and his responsibility is to it. He can function only in the here and now, and the words which unite reality and essence would be just as impossible without

[82]Buddeberg, p. 150.
[83]Steiner, p. 225.
[84]Steiner, p. 226.

this content of actuality as they are without angel essence. Our concrete world is the only home of the expressible. For this reason it has unique value, just as man has, and man's function is to lend permanence to this value by relating it to the angel world.[85] If the things of the world are not experienced with love, they vanish without transformation into invisible absolutes. This is much too often the fate of the real world in our modern culture where things are valued for their practical use alone. Their value is the temporary value of function. In the hurry of modern life man has neither the time nor the inclination to love the things he uses. He does not form an inner image (ein Bild) of them,[86] a loss for them because they vanish without being rescued into angel permanence, and a tragedy for man because his inner world shrinks into a mere vestige. The eternal essence of the inner image has been replaced by the temporary image of utility with the hardness of specificity, and hardness is characterized by brittleness. As soon as the pattern of use—the crust—changes, the utilitarian model breaks apart to be replaced by a new and likewise temporary pattern.[87] Two final images summarize the positive and negative aspects of this stanza. As parts of technology, hammers are destructive.[88] On a deeper level, man's inner world—his heart—is subjected to the hammer blows of suffering and sorrow rooted in his finiteness and his awareness of it. The beating of the heart is a physical phenomenon and stands for his existence as a physical entity. On all levels the hammers may be summarized as the finiteness of physical reality. In Rilkean terminology heart is the symbol for the inner world. Thus the symbol of the heart between the hammers encompasses both the finite external world and the infinite inner world. In the second image the teeth stand for the same negative forces of destruction as the hammer, and the tongue performs the same function as the heart in praising life as meaningful and valuable and in pronouncing words in such a way that they are a unity of essence and existence.

What then can man take before the angel in his praise? He cannot take emotion, for that exists perfectly in the angel world and only imperfectly in the human one. He can show the angel the world of things, of physical reality, which is uniquely his and which the angel can know only in the

[85]Steiner, p. 231.
[86]Guardini, p. 351.
[87]Guardini, p. 355.
[88]Guardini, pp. 355–56.

transformed state of man's inner world. Such simple objects as pottery or rope which are made with love by hand and which become part of us by continual use and love are as astonishing to the angel as the perfection of the angel absolute is to us. Like the creature world, the things are innocent and happy, because having no awareness of death, they exist in simple sponta-

60 neous harmony. Man, who knows death and therefore sorrow, experiences sorrow not as an abstract emotion but in relation to what he loves; he knows sorrow and grief when something or someone he loves perishes. The world of things can thus unknowingly represent human sorrow. Yet even when the things perish in actuality, they survive beyond the sound of the violin in the angel world if they have undergone transformation by man. So the world of things looks to man for rescue, even though his existence is no more permanent than theirs, perhaps even less so, for he alone is aware of death. Paradoxically when a perishable object in finite time enters through love into finite man's inner being, a unity is attained which transcends the limitations of time and space to enter the angel world.

67 The next to last section summarizes man's task, his acceptance of it, and the resultant view of life as meaningful. Transformation into an absolute is the wish, the dream, and the commission of earth. As springtime transforms the earth and gives it new life, so the individual joyfully accepts the task of giving the things of the earth new life in taking them into his inner world. But now he has moved beyond seeing nature as a pattern, which implies a subject-object relationship, to a unity with it where death has ceased to be the mutually exclusive opposite of life and is an everpresent part of life as transformation rather than final end—a note which will be repeated at the close of the tenth elegy.

77 The final section returns to the question of the meaning of life. It is the final answer to the opening "why" of this elegy. Life is no less transient than before. Neither the innate unity of childhood nor awareness of death as the ultimate future are lessened. Yet as the previous section has shown, man's unique role of transformation of actuality shows him that he is a necessary part of an all-encompassing whole where death is transformation rather than end. He can now affirm life together with death as part of that life as abundant, desirable, and meaningful. The negative aspect of life as limitation has been sublimated into an affirmation of life as uniquely valuable within its finite limits. Although man belongs to the finite and passing world of physical reality because he is an existing physical entity, he also

relates to the angel world of the absolute through the unbounded inner world of his heart. Only man stands on the threshold between these two worlds and in relating them to each other enhances each with the other. Here lies the strip of fertile soil for which the second elegy longed.

The first fifteen lines of the tenth elegy were written at Duino early in 1912, expanded in 1913 in Paris, and completed in Muzot on 11 February 1922. It summarizes the ideas of the entire cycle in an extremely compact and cryptic symbolism. To probe the depth and complexity of the concepts and images requires beyond factual knowledge a deeply individual intuitive receptivity, making critical commentary extraordinarily hazardous. At best only a few of the myriad possibilities can be pointed out, and each reader must supplement them by response from within himself.

The beginning section continues and summarizes the theme of the ninth elegy, a view of life wherein death is sublimated into transformation of life within an eternal universe so that it ceases to function as a final barrier or end, and life becomes more open. Only when man can see and accept death as a part of life itself can he truly praise life. He cannot genuinely praise it and find joy in it until he can acknowledge, understand, and accept all of it, the negative limitations as well as the positive possibilities, the suffering and sorrow as well as the joy. Life is pictured as a musical instrument with the hammers of the heart from the ninth elegy—the beating of the heart and the cares and sorrows which beat upon man—now striking the strings of a stringed musical instrument to produce the sounds of joy and praise in the second line. But if man is unprepared, uncertain, or weak—if the strings are not taut or slip or break—he can produce only off-key or glissando notes, not the true, clear notes of joy and praise. From the musical imagery Rilke turns to the hammers of sorrow and their significance for human life. Joy and sorrow are parts of the same whole as life and death.[89] Complete acceptance of the role of sorrow in life without any reservations brings with it the radiance of joy, which being rooted in totality, transcends brief, restricted happiness. Authentic sorrow is the very basis of life itself, for it is inherent in the limitations imposed by the fact of corporeal existence, and therefore inconsolable. The submissive acceptance of such sorrow implies comprehension of its necessity and complete acceptance of life which encompasses it, culminating in praise. Night has a long tradition of relation to sorrow and death as the final sleep or rest. Night is the time of both greater loneliness and greater openness. As contours vanish in the darkness,

[89]Steiner, p. 247.

124

the world becomes less finite, less bounded, and man is more united with it. The subject-object barrier loses its distinctness, and man's separation from the external world diminishes. But as the role of physical reality decreases, so does the activity of the mind as man's mode of relationship to it, and emotion becomes freer. The longing for loved ones grows more intense and sorrow and loneliness are more pronounced. Such nights are pictured as sisters, hinting at the feminine gender of the German word for "night" and at mythological images where sorrow is portrayed by female figures. The tradition of loosened hair as a symbol of sorrow is older than written human history, as we know from Biblical records. But man tries to avoid sorrow; he wastes it and thereby loses knowledge and acceptance of life as bounded. Instead of embracing sorrow he tries to elude it. When it becomes unavoidable, he wishes for it to end and ponders how long it might endure. He squanders sorrow by failing to comprehend its nature, role, and necessity. All else in life comes and goes, but it remains with us as long as life itself. It is thus the evergreen of life because it endures, darker than other plants, symbolizing finiteness and death as inseparable components of life. If life is seen as a year—mysterious because we cannot forsee the cycle—sorrow is the winter season. Man must understand that in life's winter season of sorrow as in nature's winter new life is developing unseen beneath the surface. Winter and sorrow are not termination but only a necessary stage in the never-ending cycle from which new life continually springs. Sorrow is an outpost of life, a far outer limit which forces man to ponder the nature and meaning of life and gain richer perception of it in his knowledge that suffering and sorrow are inseparable from life itself. In any authentic mode of living sorrow is to be valued as the very soil and dwelling place of human life, not to be wasted in attempted avoidance.[90]

The first seven lines of the second section are concerned with the squandering of grief in the image of the City of Grief. Beginning with *The Book of Hours*, Rilke uses the city to symbolize what is false, and here, too, the city connotes inauthentic and superficial life. In such life grief is expressed in ostentatious mourning, in the empty, hushed, funereal silence which is considered the proper expression of grief.[91] This silence is an outward form prescribed by convention as the suitable expression of loss, a fitting reaction

[90]Steiner, pp. 249–50.
[91]Kreutz, p. 140.

to the death represented by Madame Lamort in the fifth elegy. Such grief is empty and meaningless because it is imposed from without, not organically
*17* developed from within. Since this death—the mold—is empty, the resulting casting—the grief—is likewise empty. Such grief advertises its existence in hushed silence, dolorous music—the gilded noise—and elaborate and
*20* expensive gravestones. It is administered by the church in proper and prescribed ritual, neat and religious, but of no real meaning or solace to those who pay for it. In bounding such sorrow, the church closes off the view of it as an inherent part of life and distorts comprehension of it.[92] It is as frustrating and useless as a post office closed and nonfunctioning on Sunday[93] or like a bargain sale of useless and discarded merchandise. Such outward pretense is a function of the world of physical reality, an expression of possessive love of an object, and it forms no link to the angel absolute. It is grief as meaningless and fleeting as the life which produces it and as empty as its expression in outer form and pretense.

*23*    The following eleven lines to the break indicated by the series of dots characterize the life which is the source of such grief. As the theme of grief was related to the death symbolized by Madame Lamort in the fifth elegy, inauthentic life is described as a carnival, the world of the acrobats in the same elegy. Those who live the carnival life like to imagine that they are free to form their lives, that they are masters of their own destinies capable of rising to the heights of success by their own effort. Yet this is only a delusion because man by his very existence as a living thing in the world of
*24* physical reality cannot be completely free. His imagined freedom is like a swing which not only rises but also falls, as all life must also fall in death. The ordinary view of life as a rising curve and death as a falling curve is embodied in the curve of the path of the swing which only appears different because it is inverted. The attractions of this carnival include divers and jugglers of eagerness—human eagerness to reach the heights of success and plumb the depths of experience; but as Steiner points out, both always return to the surface without having accomplished or acquired anything of enduring value.[94] The actions of the divers and jugglers are empty virtuoso performances lacking inner stability. The shooting gallery of good

[92]Steiner, p. 251.
[93]Kreutz, p. 141.
[94]Steiner, p. 253.

fortune or luck emphasizes the role of external reality in the search for wealth, success, and happiness, the usual human goals which are applauded and envied by one's neighbors. But since they are external goals, they are vulnerable to external circumstances over which the individual has no control. Even those who are skilled in the pursuit of such goals are subject to their inherent unpredictability, and when by chance one does hit the target, its tinny sound advertises its falseness.[95] Yet it is the nature of man to stagger on, replacing one unsatisfying, temporary goal with another, reeling from carnival booth to carnival booth in his search for success. Turning to sexual symbolism Rilke describes the avidity of the adult search for material wealth, man's insatiable curiosity about how money functions because that is useful knowledge. The scurrilous terms of the description clearly reveal that for Rilke intense preoccupation with material wealth was as pornographic as preoccupation with sex.

The carnival world is bounded by the board fence surrounding the carnival; it is plastered with advertisements including one for the beer named "deathless." Such life tries to shut out awareness of death, as if refusing to acknowledge its existence would make it go away. This can be achieved only when one is continually distracted by new goals and activities; the deceivingly sweet taste of the beer of deathlessness only masks its true bitterness.[96]

Just beyond the planks, outside the carnival world, is the real world. Here are found three groups which stand for a view of the universe as a harmonious unity—children and animals from the innate unity of the creature world and lovers. Although this is genuine existence in contrast to the delusion of the carnival, it is still limited as the sparseness of the grass informs us.[97] The unity of this world with the absolute world of the hereafter is revealed by the structural unity of this portion. The lament—sorrow and death as inseparable parts of life—appears within life; and in following her, the youth crosses the threshold of the subject-object barrier to conscious awareness of death. He follows the lament, for he senses her nobility and significance for life, but he cannot follow her beyond his own world. Being bound within the physical world, he can know sorrow and suffering only

[95]Kreutz, p. 142.
[96]Guardini, p. 383.
[97]Kreutz, p. 143.

as it appears there, not as it is in the absolute world where it is at home. Yet its appearance in both worlds attests to the validity of its role in human life and to the validity of the life in this section. The long second section thus moves through the world of the living from the City of Grief, to the carnival of life which produces such grief, to the genuine but limited life beyond the carnival, to the appearance of genuine sorrow within such life in the symbol of the lament.

47    The third section moves beyond the actual world of the living to the imagined world of the hereafter. Although this is the world where the angel and the absolute are at home, they do not appear, for the remainder of the tenth elegy is devoted to the significance of the hereafter for human life, and no attempt is made to describe or define the essentially indefinable. In keeping with Rilke's concept of the universe as dynamic, our guide, a dead youth, leads us through a number of levels or layers, each further removed from the actual world than the one which precedes it. This theme was introduced in the first elegy where the dead find their new world strange, where they must work at catching up in order to begin to sense eternity. This is the situation at the beginning of the third section where the dead youth is met by a young lament at the border of the land of sorrow. The dead youth could signify those who die young in the earlier elegies. It might also indicate the level of development of the dead within their new world where they are beginners and where the youth learns that sorrow is the connecting link between life and death. Genuine life is dominated by death, as the lament appeared in such life in the preceding section. The jewels of the

50    young lament are sorrow, and she is veiled in patient endurance. She shows these to girls who are closer to love and its concomitant sorrow than men. The youths, too, exist in a state of complete harmony in this new world, for her silence with them signifies sublimation of the dichotomies of life into perfect unity.

54    As human life in the ninth elegy is lived in the valley, the home of the lament in the fourth section is located in the valley of the realm of the hereafter. Here an older lament—a further stage of development—replaces the initial guide. She tells the dead youth of the former role of sorrow in human life, that in past times their race was richer and greater, more esteemed in the human world. The seventh elegy has shown that only what is transformed within the human heart in the real world enters the absolute world of the hereafter. Since modern man tries to ignore the role of suffer-

ing and death in life, this area of the absolute world is likewise impoverished. The full intensity of sorrow and anger now are experienced only rarely in the human world, and both worlds are poorer because of it.

61   The older lament continues her tour of their land, showing the dead youth the ruins of temples connoting the former vital role of religion in bridging the here and the hereafter before it deteriorated into mere ritual, and the remnants of fortresses standing for the former dominance of life by free acknowledgement and willing acceptance of suffering, sorrow, and death in life. The tears which in the first section lend radiance to the human face flourish here as trees with their connotations of beauty and organic harmony, linking in their verticality heaven and earth, man and angel.[98] Sadness, which appears in life as a delicate plant, perhaps one of the ever-greens which symbolize death for us, here covers fields with flowering abundance. The creature world with its innate oneness appears as contentedly grazing herds and flocks, and the birds of the seventh and eighth elegies now combine the sensory impressions of sight and sound into perfect unity.

The second portion of this section turns to night with all its attributes of love, openness, and starry sky. The graves of the heroes of the land of lament emphasize that even here in the realm of eternity there is change and end. The sibyls and prophets represented for earlier ages mystical wisdom which could bridge the worlds of the here and the hereafter and thus erase the bounds of earthly time and space. Our present age denies this ability, and so the sibyls and prophets are dead in the absolute world as well as in our own. After visiting these graves there arises in the night a sphinx, the brother of the Egyptian one, for this is the absolute world, and only the non-corporeal absolute image can exist here.[99] It combines the concept of man in its human face with death in its role as burial chamber.[100] Physically the sphinx seems to tower to the very stars, and by elevating the human countenance to the universally valid stars, the sphinx signifies the validity of man's unique role and meaning in the universe in spite of his mortality.[101]

The following section continues the imagery of the sphinx. The double crown signifies the duality of human life combined into a single crown. The

[98]Guardini, p. 397.
[99]Steiner, p. 268.
[100]Buddeberg, p. 177.
[101]Guardini, p. 404.

129

owl which flies from the edge of the crown stands for both wisdom and death. The full curve of the cheek reminds us of life and also of ripe fruit which contains within it the seed of death. The image of the owl brushing along the cheek thus visualizes life and death as a unity and highlights Rilke's belief that only awareness of death can give true understanding of

85  life and its meaning. As in the previous section, the cry of the bird and the path of flight, which in the real world would be separate in their sensory appeal, are united in perception of the auditory stimulus by the eye in the first image, and in perception of the visual symbol by the ear in the second image, standing for the absence of the subject-object barrier in the hereafter.[102] The double image continues in the indescribable outline—the perfect unity of life and death which the living can only sense—sketched across the double page of the open book,[103] revealing that in the hereafter the pages of both life and death are comprehensible simultaneously.

89  From the sphinx the next section turns to the stars. These stars are described as the new ones of the land of sorrow. This does not mean that these are not the same stars which man sees in his own world, but that here in the absolute world of the hereafter where they are perfectly visible, they appear different from the ones we see distorted by the atmosphere or symbolically by our perspective vision. They are valid in both the divided world of man and the totality of the angel and stand for the presence of the absolute within our own limited world, for the eternal within our temporal realm.

90  The first star, the Rider, could stand for man's perception of life and death as a duality which is imposed upon him by his corporeity, though in sensing a unity which he can never truly know he attains a semblance of unity as do the horse and rider. The Staff may be a symbol for life's finiteness, for, like the traveler at the close of the eighth elegy, man inexorably moves through

92  life, always taking leave of what was but is no more for him. The Wreath of Fruit is related to the strip of fertile soil which man seeks in the second elegy, to life as fruit bearing within it the seed of death, and to the role of man's heart as bridge between the real and the angel worlds. As a circle the wreath stands for completeness and unity. The Cradle possibly symbolizes childhood as a mode of existence of innate unity with the universe. The Road may stand for man's journey through life as a journey into openness rather

---

[102]Buddeberg, p. 176. See also the Rilke letter quoted below in Appendix C, pp. 138–39.
[103]Steiner, pp. 272–73.

than a journey to death as final end.[104] The Burning Book combines transformation and change in the image of burning with the permanence of the book and can stand for the "word" of the ninth elegy which embodies both the existence and essence of what it expresses. The Puppet or Doll may represent man's patient endurance of life as a surface phenomenon, like the acrobats in the fifth elegy, until it suddenly acquires meaning, as symbolized by the appearance of the angel in the fourth elegy. The Window possibly points to love as man's opening to self-transcendence, to a view of life unbounded by object vision, and to the inner world of the human heart as an opening between the angel and human worlds. The Mothers recall the third elegy and the role of womanhood. Mothers represent complete acceptance of life and its myriad possibilities within its inherent limitations, the openness of love, and confidence in the meaningfulness of life which they impart to others through love.

The youth must continue on his journey through the land of sorrow, and the lament shows him the spring of joy. Its location in the land of sorrow emphasizes the unity of joy and sorrow in the same way life and death are a unity. Joy is affirmation of all life as meaningful, including the ultimate limitation of death within it. But what appears in the hereafter as a modest spring—yet significant as source and beginning—flows through the human world as a navigable river. But since true joy springs from sorrow and includes foreknowledge of death, the river remains unused. Man's search for joy deteriorates into a search for goal-directed happiness which plays a false and exaggerated role in human life.

From the spring of joy the dead youth continues into the mountains of primeval sorrow alone. He has reached the limit of human perception[105] and we can accompany him no farther. The blackness of the night and the soundlessness of his footsteps signify the complete boundlessness of this world which is indiscernible to man, beyond man's ability even to sense or imagine it and its perfect harmony. It is the realm of the infinitely dead.

The final sections return to the world of the living and summarize the meaning of the elegies and the meaning of life and death in two poetic images—the image of the empty hanging catkins on the hazel bush in spring and the image of the falling spring rain. Both are images of spring

[104]Steiner, p. 280.
[105]Buddeberg, p. 181.

with all its promise of an end to the dormancy of winter and birth of new life.[106] Both are characterized by a downward curve symbolizing their ultimate end like the rising jet of the fountain in the seventh elegy which contains within itself its predictable fall. The two concluding symbols thus stand for life and death as a unity and death as transformation, for the hazel bush will continue to produce life after the dormancy of winter, and the rain will bring forth the new life of spring and summer.

For man this signifies that although life appears to end in the ultimate limitation of death, it must be welcomed as positive in value—even the falling curve acquires positive value as an innate function of totality.[107] For those who recognize life and death as part of the same unity, the falling curve of life terminates not in nothingness, but in never-ending totality. Death has been sublimated into life, not as Dionysian continuation, but as transformation of a finite object within an eternal whole.

[106]Kreutz, p. 151.

[107]Bernhard Blume, "Das Motiv des Fallens bei Rilke," *Modern Language Notes*, 60 (1945), 298.

# APPENDIX A

Witold Hulewicz translated Rilke's works into Polish. Needing assistance for his translation of the *Elegies*, he had written Rilke requesting information about their meaning. Rilke gave him his only interpretation of this work in a letter dated 13 November 1925 (*Briefe*, II, 478–85) and postmarked Sierre, which begins with a series of questions and Rilke's answers to them. This translation begins with the fourth question, since the first three are not concerned with the *Elegies*.

Here, dear friend, I myself scarcely dare to say anything. In connection with the poems themselves some explanations could be attempted, but this way? Where would one begin?

And am *I* the one to venture to give the correct interpretation of the Elegies? They reach infinitely beyond me. I consider them a further elaboration of those basic premises which were already presented in the "Book of Hours," which playfully and experimentally use a cosmology in both parts of the "New Poems," and which then conflictingly condensed in "Malte" revert into life and very nearly lead to proof that this life extending into the unfathomable is impossible. In the "Elegies" life in the same circumstances once again becomes possible, indeed it experiences here that ultimate *affirmation* which the young Malte still could not attain, even though he was on the correct and difficult road of "des longues études." *In the "Elegies" affirmation of life and of death proves to be the same thing.* What is experienced and praised here is that to affirm the one without the other in the last analysis would be a limitation excluding everything infinite. *Death* is the *side of life* turned away from us, the side unilluminated by us: we must seek to realize the broadest conception of our existence which is at home in *both unbounded realms, is nourished inexhaustibly from both* . . . The true configuration of life extends through *both* realms, the blood of the most comprehensive cycle circulates through both: *there is neither a here nor a hereafter, but only the great unity* in which the superior beings, the "angels," are at home. And now the place of the problem of love in this world expanded by its larger half, in this world only now *complete* and *unified*. I am amazed that the "Sonnets to Orpheus," which are every bit as "weighty" and filled with the same essence, are not more helpful to you in understanding the "Elegies." The latter were begun in 1912 (at Duino), continued—fragmentarily—in Spain and Paris until 1914; the war completely interrupted this my greatest work when in 1922 I (here) ventured to take them up again, the "Sonnets to Orpheus" (which were *not* part of my plan) were dictated to me stormily within a few days and preceded the new elegies and their conclusion. They are of the same "birth" as the "Elegies," as cannot be otherwise, and that they suddenly surfaced without my will in connection with a girl who died young brings them even closer to the source of their origin; this link is one more connection to the center of *that* realm whose depth and influence, everywhere unbounded, we share with the dead and with future generations. We, living in the here and now, are not for one moment satisfied in the temporal world nor limited to it; again and again we pass over to earlier generations, to our origin, and to those who apparently will follow us. In that most comprehensive *"boundless"* world everyone *exists*, one cannot say "simultaneously," for the suspension of time requires that they all *exist*. Frailty everywhere rushes into profound being. And so all formations of what exists here are to be used not as temporally bounded only, but so far as we are able are to be transposed into those higher spheres of meaning in which we share. But *not in the Christian sense* (from which I am moving more and more emphatically away), but in an intense and blessed awareness, that what is seen and touched *here* is to be transposed into the broader, the very broadest sphere. Not into the other world, the shadow of which darkens the earth, but into a totality, into *the totality*. Nature, the things we associate with and use, are frail and temporary things; yet as long as we are here, they are *our* possessions and our friends, sharing cognizance of our limitations and joy, as they have been the confidants of our forefathers. So it is a matter of not regarding everything earthly with disfavor or disparaging it, but precisely because of its fragility which it shares with us, these phenomena and things should be comprehended and transformed by us in most intense understanding. Transformed? Yes, for it is our task to imprint this frail and unenduring earth so passionately and ardently in us that its essence is resurrected "invisibly" within us. *We are the bees of the invisible world. Nous butinons éperdument le miel du visible, pour l'accumuler dans la grande ruche d'or de l'invisible.* [*We perpetually gather the honey of the visible world in order to store it in the great golden hive of the invisible one.*] The "Elegies" show us at this work, the work of this continual transformation of the beloved visible and comprehensible world into the invisible vibration and stimulation of our nature, which introduces new frequencies of vibration into the universal spheres of vibration. (Since the various substances in the universe are only different rates of vibration, we make in this manner not only intensities of a mental variety, but who knows, new objects, metals, nebulae and constellations.) And this activity is strangely enhanced and urged on by the increasingly rapid disappearance of so much that is visible which no longer will be replaced. Even for our grandparents a "house," a "fountain," a tower familiar to them, even their own clothing, their coat: these things were infinitely more to them, infinitely more familiar; almost everything was a vessel in which they found human elements present and stored up human elements. Now empty, neutral things crowd over from America, superficial things, *appurtenances of life* . . . A house in the American sense, an American apple or a grape vine from there has *nothing* in common with the house, the fruit, the grape, into which the hope and contemplation of our forefathers had entered . . . The animated, the perceived things sharing cognizance with us are declining and can no longer be replaced. *We are perhaps the last who have still known such things.* On us rests the responsibility not only to preserve their memory (that would be little and unreliable), but also their human and laral value. ("Laral" in the sense of household deities.) The earth has no other refuge than to become invisible: *in us*, we who share in the invisible world with part of our nature, (at least) have shares in it, and who during our life here on earth can increase what belongs to us by adding invisibility—*in us* alone can this intimate and continual transformation of the visible world into invisibility which is no longer dependent on being visible and tangible be carried out, as our own destiny continually becomes more intensely *present and invisible* at the same time. The *Elegies* set up this standard for life: they assert, they celebrate this awareness. They set it carefully into its traditions by laying claim to very ancient traditions and reports of traditions for this supposition, and even in the Egyptian cult of the dead the "Elegies" invoke a sense of such connections. (Although the "Land of Lament" through which the older "Lament" leads the dead youth is *not to be equated* with Egypt, but only to a certain extent with a reflection of the land of the Nile in the desert clarity of the consciousness of the dead.) When one makes the mistake of clinging to the *Catholic* conception of death, the hereafter and eternity in the Elegies or Sonnets, then one strays completely from their point of origin and prepares the way for even more basic errors. The "angel" of the Elegies has nothing to do with the angel of the Christian heaven (more nearly with the angel figures of Islam) . . . The angel of the *Elegies* is that creation in which the transformation of the visible world into invisibility which we carry out appears already completed. For the angel of the Elegies all earlier towers and bridges are existing, *because* they long have been invisible, and the still standing towers and bridges of our existence are *already* invisible, although (for us) still physically present. The angel of the Elegies is that being which stands for the idea of recognizing a higher order of reality in invisibility.—Therefore "awesome" to us because we, his lovers and trans-formers, still cling to visible reality.—All the worlds of the universe are rushing into invisibility as their next deeper reality; *a few stars literally grow more intense and perish in the boundless awareness of the angels—*, *others are allotted to beings which transform them slowly and with difficulty, in whose terror and ecstasy they attain their nearest invisible reality. We are,* let it be emphasized once more, *we are in the sense of the Elegies these transformers of the earth; our entire existence, the soaring and plunging of our love, all this fits us for this task* (in addition to which basically no other exists). (The Sonnets portray details of this activity which appears here under the name and patronage of a deceased maiden whose immaturity and innocence hold open the door of the grave so that having entered, she belongs to those powers which keep the life half of totality fresh and open toward the other vulnerable half.) The Elegies and the Sonnets contribute mutually to each other—, and I see an infinite blessing in the fact that with the same breath I was enabled to fill both sails: the little rust-colored sail of the Sonnets and the gigantic white sail of the Elegies.

Dear friend, perhaps you will find here some advice and information, and beyond that help yourself along. For I do not know whether I could ever say more.

Yours,
R. M. Rilke

A letter dated 14 July 1907 (Dieter Bassermann, *Der späte Rilke*, pp. 415–16) describes an acrobatic performance by the well-known French troupe of Père Rollin. Some of the description is reflected in the fifth elegy.

I have just been in the Luxembourg; in front of it in the direction of the Pantheon Père Rollin and his troupe have set up, the same carpet is there, the same discarded coats, heavy winter coats, are heaped on a chair, on which just enough room is left so that the little son, the grandson of the old man, with his serious face, can sit a little (just as much as is necessary for it to be sitting) between performances. Everything is just like it was a year ago. But Père Rollin who used to swing heavy weights about, no longer performs and doesn't say a word. He is set on drumming. Pathetically patiently he stands there with his great strength which no longer is put to proper use, although it is still a little too much for drumming. He drums much too often, then his son-in-law whistles at him and startled, he quits and asks forgiveness with a movement of his heavy shoulders and shifts his weight ceremoniously to the other foot. But the next moment he must be whistled at again, the old man: he is drumming again. He is scarcely aware of it. He could drum forever; they shouldn't think that he would get tired. But it is not his son-in-law who is in charge now; to be sure he performs well, there's nothing to be said about that, and he likes to, as he must. But the one who runs everything, and *how*, is naturally his daughter, it's in her blood. The weights have been sold, they are no longer in style, and the children are up-to-date. But they have come up with some marvelous ideas; the old man is happy. And the way she speaks, his daughter, so quick-witted and sturdy almost like him, the old Père Rollin himself, whom no one surpassed, not in wit and not in his performance. Among the spectators were some who knew him: Hey, Père Rollin! But he only nods preoccupied; drumming is important business and he takes it seriously.

# APPENDIX C

In a letter dated 1 February 1914 (Rilke, *Briefwechsel mit Benvenuta*, pp. 22–23) Rilke wrote of his journey to Egypt in January, February, and March, 1911. Many of the references recur in the tenth elegy.

My friend, in Berlin take a look at the bust of Amenophis the Fourth in the center glass-roofed pavilion of the Egyptian Museum (I could tell you much about this king); sense from this face what it means to be face to face with the infinite world and in such a limited surface to create a balance with the entire figure by means of the accentuated arrangement of a few features. Couldn't one turn away from a starry night to find in this countenance the same law flourishing, the same greatness, depth and incomprehensibility? I have learned to observe from such things, and when later in Egypt they stood before me in great numbers, in their very own nature, comprehension of them swept over me in such waves that I lay almost an entire night facing of the great Sphinx as though cast out from all my life in its presence. You see, I haven't gotten to music yet, but I'm familiar with noises, and one of the strangest came to me there; shall I tell you about it?
You undoubtedly know that it is difficult to be alone in that place; it has become a completely public place; the most fortuitous foreigners are dragged there in droves;—yet I had skipped the evening meal: even the Arabs sat at a distance around their fire; I had gotten rid of one of them who had noticed me by buying two oranges from him; and moreover the darkness protected me from being seen. I had waited for darkness out in the desert, then I came in slowly with the Sphinx to my back and calculated that the moon would have to come up behind the nearest pyramid now bathed intensely in the light of the sunset, for it was full moon. And when I had finally walked around the pyramid, the moon not only stood rather high in the sky, it poured such a flood of moonlight over the endless view that I had to shade my eyes from its light with my hand in order to find my way between the boulders and the excavations.—The back part of the body of the Sphinx does not rise significantly above the plain of sand, for since the first excavations it has been covered over again several times, and up to now it has been considered satisfactory to keep the front side free up to the paws so that removal of the ground results in a downward slope toward the Sphinx resembling half a funnel. On this steep slope facing the gigantic figure I sought a place and lay wrapped in my coat, in fear, endlessly communing. I do not know whether I was ever so completely conscious of my life as in those night hours in which it lost all value: for what was it compared to all this? The level on which it was played out grew dark, everything that is world and life proceeded on a higher stage on which a constellation and a God lingered silently. You also will remember

having experienced this: that the view of a scene, of the ocean, of the endlessly starry night imbues us with the conviction of connections and insights which we are not able to comprehend: this is precisely what I experienced here very intensely; here there arose a figure which was oriented toward heaven; on which the millennia had produced nothing but a little disdainful decay, and it was completely unimaginable that this thing bore human features (the completely recognizable features of a human face) and that in its exalted position they sufficed. Oh, dear friend, I told myself that this, this which we alternately leave to destiny and take into our own hands, must be capable of signifying something great if its form can endure in such surroundings. This face had assumed the habits of space, individual portions of its gaze and of its smile had been destroyed, but the rising and setting of the heavens had reflected upon it enduring feelings. From time to time I closed my eyes and although my heart pounded, I reproached myself with not feeling this deeply enough: did I not have to reach a point in my astonishment where I had never been before? I said to myself: just imagine you had been carried here with eyes blindfolded and put down here obliquely in the deep, scarcely blowing coolness and now you open your eyes . . . And when I actually opened them now, good heavens,—it took a good while before they recovered, comprehended that creature, the mouth, the cheek, the forehead on which moonlight and shadow flowed from expression to expression. How many times already had my eye attempted this detailed cheek; up there it rounded so gently, as if there were room for *more* places than down here among us. And then, just as I observed it again I suddenly was drawn in an unexpected manner into its confidence, and I got to know it, then I experienced it in the most complete sensing of its roundness. Not until a moment afterward did I comprehend *what* had happened. Just imagine this: behind the protrusion of the crown on the head of the Sphinx an owl had flown up and slowly, indescribably audible in the pure depth of the night, had brushed the face with its gentle flight: and now there emerged in my hearing which had grown very sharp in the long stillness of the night the contour of that cheek, sketched there as if by a miracle.

# SELECT BIBLIOGRAPHY

## Primary Works:

Rilke, Rainer Maria. *Briefe*. 2 vols. Wiesbaden: Insel, 1950.

———. *Briefe aus den Jahren 1914–1921*. Leipzig: Insel, 1938.

———. *Briefwechsel mit Benvenuta*. Eßlingen: Bechtle, 1954.

———. *Sämtliche Werke*. 6 vols. Wiesbaden: Insel, 1955–1966.

## English Translations of the *Duineser Elegien*:

Rilke, Rainer Maria. *The Duino Elegies*. English Translation by Harry Behn. Mt. Vernon, N.Y.: Peter Pauper Press, 1957.

———. *The Duino Elegies*. English Translation with Introduction and Commentary by Stephen Garmey and Jay Wilson. New York: Harper and Row, 1972.

———. *Duino Elegies*. Translated by Jessie Lamont. New York: The Fine Editions Press, 1945.

———. *Duino Elegies.* German Text with English Translation, Introduction, and Commentary by J. B. Leishman and Stephen Spender. London: Hogarth Press, 1939.

———. *Duino Elegies*. German Text with English Translation and Introduction by C. F. MacIntyre. Berkeley: University of California Press, 1963.

———. "Rilke's First Duino Elegy." Translated by George Nordmeyer. *Germanic Review*, 27 (1952), 243–45.

———. *Elegies of Duino*. English Translation by Nora Purtscher-Wydenbruck. Vienna: Amandus, 1948.

———. ["The Elegies."] English Translation by David Young. *Field* 5 (1971), 56–71; 6 (1972), 63–76; 7 (1972), 24–37; 8 (1973), 36–51; 9 (1973), 55–70.

## Critical Works:

Allemann, Beda. *Zeit und Figur beim späten Rilke*. [Pfullingen]: Neske, [1961].

Andreas-Salomé, Lou. *Lebensrückblick*. Zürich: Max Niehans, 1951.

───. *Rainer Maria Rilke*. Leipzig: Insel, 1928.

Angelloz, J. F. *Les Elégies de Duino*. Traduites et commentées par J. F. Angelloz. Paris: P. Hartmann, 1936.

Barker, Orus C. "Cosmic Play: Rainer Maria Rilke's Understanding of Man and the World," (Duke, 1968) *Dissertation Abstracts*, 29 (1968/69): 3125 A.

Bassermann, Dieter. "Engel und Orpheus: Anmerkungen zu Rainer Maria Rilkes Elegien und Sonetten," *Die neue Rundschau*, 50 (1939), 331–48.

───. *Der späte Rilke*. Munich: Leibniz, 1947.

Belmore, H. W. *Rilke's Craftsmanship*. Oxford: Basil Blackwell, 1954.

Bergel, Kurt. "Childhood and Love in Rilke's Fourth Duino Elegy," *Germanic Review*, 21 (1946), 48–54.

───. "Rilke's Fourth Duino Elegy and Kleist's Essay über das Marionetten-theater," *Modern Language Notes*, 60 (1945), 73–78.

Blanckenhagen, Peter H. von. "Picasso and Rilke. 'La Famille des Saltim-banques,' " *Measure*, 1 (1950), 165–85.

Blume, Bernhard. "Das Motiv des Fallens bei Rilke," *Modern Language Notes*, 60 (1945), 295–302.

Bollnow, Otto Friedrich. *Rilke*. Stuttgart: Kohlhammer, 1951.

Boney, Elaine E. "The Concept of Being in Rilke's *Elegies*," *Symposium*, 15 (1961), 12–21.

───. "Existentialist Thought in the Works of Rainer Maria Rilke," (Texas, 1958) *Dissertation Abstracts*, 19 (1958/59), 1750.

───. "Rilke's Concept of Art." *Homage to Charles Blaise Qualia*. Ed. John Dowling. Lubbock: Texas Technological College Press, 1962, pp. 65–74.

Brecht, Franz Josef. *Schicksal und Auftrag des Menschen. Philosophische Interpreta-tionen zu Rilkes Duineser Elegien*. Basel: Reinhardt, 1949.

Browning, Robert M. "Rilke's 'Madame Lamort' and Leopardi's 'Dialogo della moda e della morte,' " *Symposium*, 7 (1953), 358–62.

Buddeberg, Else. *Denken und Dichten des Seins: Heidegger, Rilke*. Stuttgart: Metzler, 1956.

————. *Die Duineser Elegien R. M. Rilkes.* Karlsruhe: Stahlberg, 1948.

————. *Kunst und Existenz im Spätwerk Rilkes. Eine Darstellung nach seinen Briefen.* Karlsruhe: Stahlberg, 1948.

————. *Rainer Maria Rilke, eine innere Biographie.* Stuttgart: Metzler, 1954.

Butler, E. M. *Rainer Maria Rilke.* Cambridge: Cambridge University Press, 1946.

Cämmerer, Heinrich. *Rainer Maria Rilkes Duineser Elegien: Deutung der Dichtung.* Stuttgart: Metzler, 1937.

————. "Zur Siebenten Duineser Elegie: Deutung der Elegie," *Dichtung und Volkstum,* 37 (1936), 60–66.

Cassierer-Solnitz, Eva. *Das Stundenbuch R. M. Rilkes. Die Aufzeichnungen des Malte Laurids Brigge. Die Duineser Elegien. Die Sonette an Orpheus. Die Götter bei Rilke.* Heidelberg: Koester, 1957.

Cutler, Anthony. "Acrobats and Angels: Art and Poetry in the Cubist Period," *Emory University Quarterly,* 20 (1964), 52–56.

Davidson, E. "Duino Elegies," *Yale Review, N.S.,* 29 (1938/39), 171–75.

Dehn, Fritz. "Rilke: Die vierte Duineser Elegie." *Gedicht und Gedanke.* Halle: Niemeyer, 1942, pp. 318–34.

Destro, Alberto. *Le Duineser Elegien e la poesia di Rainer Maria Rilke. Testo e commento dello Duineser Elegien.* Rome: Mario Bulzoni, 1970.

Fausset, Hugh I'Anson. "The Death Theme in Rilke's Life and Poetry." *Poets and Pundits.* New Haven: Yale University Press, 1947, pp. 155–69.

Ferreiro Alemparte, Jaime. "La primera elegía del Duino de Rainer Maria Rilke," *La Torre,* 25 (1959), 127–58.

————. "La segunda Elegía de Duino," *Cuadernos de Poesía española,* June 1960.

Fingerhut, Karl-Heinz. *Das Kreatürliche im Werke Rainer Maria Rilkes.* Bonn: Bouvier, 1970.

Fleischer, Margo. "Nietzsche und Rilkes Duineser Elegien." Diss. Cologne, 1958.

Fülleborn, Ulrich. *Das Strukturproblem der späten Lyrik Rilkes: Voruntersuchungen zu einem historischen Rilke-Verständnis.* Heidelberg: Winter, 1960.

Graff, W. L. *Rainer Maria Rilke: Creative Anguish of a Modern Poet.* Princeton: Princeton University Press, 1956.

―――. *Rilkes lyrische Summen*. Berlin: DeGruyter, 1960.

Guardini, Romano. *Rainer Maria Rilkes Deutung des Daseins*. Munich: Kösel, 1953.

―――. *Rilke's Duino Elegies: An Interpretation*. Translated by K. G. Knight. London: Darwen Finlayson, 1961.

―――. "Rilkes Elegienfragment 'Laß dir, daß Kindheit war . . .' " *Sprache, Dichtung, Deutung*. Würzburg: Werkbund-Verlag, 1962, pp. 35–72.

Günther, Werner. *Weltinnenraum: Die Dichtung Rainer Maria Rilkes*. Bern and Leipzig: Haupt, 1943.

Hattingberg, Magda von. *Rilke and Benvenuta*. Translated by Cyrus Brooks. New York: W. W. Norton, 1949.

Hecht, Roger. "Rilke in Translation," *Sewanee Review*, 71 (1963), 513–22.

Heerikhuizen, F. W. van. *Rainer Maria Rilke: His Life and Work*. Translated from the Dutch by F. G. Renier and A. Cliff. London: Routledge and Kegan Paul, 1951.

Heller, Erich. "Die Reise der Kunst ins Innere," *Merkur*, 19 (1965), 20–34.

Herzberg, Frederick. *Work and the Nature of Man*. Cleveland and New York: The World Publishing Co., 1966.

Hickman, Hans. "Rilke et l'Egypte," *Revue du Caire*, 20 (1957), 63–76.

Hoeniger, F. D. "Symbolism and Pattern in Rilke's Duino Elegies," *German Life and Letters*, N. S., 3 (1949/50), 271–83.

Holthusen, Hans Egon. *Portrait of Rilke*. Translated by W. H. Hargreaves. New York: Herder and Herder, 1971.

―――. *Rainer Maria Rilke: A Study of His Later Poetry*. Translated by J. B. Stern. New Haven: Yale University Press, 1952.

―――. *Der späte Rilke*. Zürich: Arche, 1949.

Huder, Walter. "Umkehr der Räume: Ein Beitrag zur Erkenntnis der Spätdichtung R. M. Rilkes," *Welt und Wort*, 13 (1958), 203–06.

Isler, E. P. "La structure des Elégies de Duino de Rainer Maria Rilke," *Les langues modernes*, 35 (1937), 225–48.

Jaeger, Hans. "Die Entstehung der fünften Duineser Elegie Rilkes," *Dichtung und Volkstum*, 40 (1939), 213–36.

Jászi, Andrew O. "Rilkes *Duineser Elegien* und die Einsamkeit," *University of California Publications in Modern Philology*, 36 (1952), 185–92.

Jayne, Richard. *The Symbolism of Space and Motion in the Works of Rainer Maria Rilke*. Frankfurt am Main: Athenäum, 1972.

Jokostra, Peter. "Nach den 'Duineser Elegien': Zum 30. Todestag," *Neue deutsche Literatur*, 4 (1956), 46–64.

Jonas, Klaus. "Die Rilke-Kritik 1950–66." *Insel Almanach auf das Jahr 1967.* Frankfurt am Main: Insel, 1966, pp. 94–121.

Kassner, Rudolf. "Gespräche mit Rilke," *Universitas*, 14 (1959), 597–602.

———. "Rainer Maria Rilke—wie ich ihn sah," *Die Zeit*, 27 December 1956, p. 6.

———. "Zen, Rilke und ich." *Geistige Welten.* [Berlin]: Ullstein, [1958], pp. 60–69.

Kippenberg, Katherina. *Rainer Maria Rilkes Duineser Elegien und Sonette an Orpheus.* Wiesbaden: Insel, 1946.

Klein, Johannes. "Die Fügung der Motive in Rilkes Duineser Elegien," *Dichtung und Volkstum*, 39 (1938), 298–314.

Kramer-Lauff, Dietgard. *Tanz und Tänzerisches in Rilkes Lyrik.* Munich: Fink, 1969.

Kommerell, Max. "Rilkes Duineser Elegien." *Gedanken über Gedichte.* Frankfurt am Main: Klostermann, 1943, pp. 491–501.

Kreutz, Heinrich. *Rilkes Duineser Elegien.* Munich: C. H. Beck, 1950.

Kunisch, Hermann. *Rainer Maria Rilke: Dasein und Dichtung.* Berlin: Duncker und Humblot, 1944.

Kunz, Marcel. *Narziß: Untersuchungen zum Werk Rainer Maria Rilkes.* Bonn: Bouvier, 1970.

Lachmann, E. "Der Engel in Rilkes *Duineser Elegien," Deutsche Vierteljahrsschrift für Literaturwissenschaft und Geistesgeschichte*, 27 (1953), 413–30.

Leishman, J. B. "Betrachtungen eines englischen Rilke-Übersetzers," *Gestalt und Gedanke: Ein Jahrbuch*, 8 (1963), 137–55.

Loose, Gerhard. "Two Notes on Rilke's *Duineser Elegien," Modern Language Notes*, 78 (1963), 430–34.

Luke, F. D. "Metaphor and Thought in Rilke's *Duino Elegies:* A Commentary on the First Elegy with a Verse Translation," *Oxford German Studies*, 2 (1967), 110–28.

Mandel, Siegfried. *Rainer Maria Rilke: The Poetic Instinct*. Carbondale and Edwardsville: Southern Illinois University Press, 1965.

Mason, Eudo C. "Kassner und Rilke," *Wort in der Zeit*, 9 No. 11 (1963), 22–32.

———. *Lebenshaltung und Symbolik bei R. M. Rilke*. Oxford: Marston, 1964.

———. *Rilke: Europe and the English-Speaking World*. London: Cambridge University Press, 1961.

———. "Rilkes magischer Existenzialismus," *Orbis Litterarum*, 11 (1956), 31–52.

Memming, Agnes K. "Der 'Bezug' als 'Grundstimmung für alles Schaffen' bei Rilke," (Pennsylvania, 1970) *Dissertation Abstracts International* 31: 5417A.

Mayer, Gerhart. *Rilke und Kassner: Eine geistige Begegnung*. Bonn: Bouvier, 1960.

Meyer, Hermann. "Die Verwandlung des Sichtbaren: Die Bedeutung der modernen bildenden Kunst für Rilkes späte Dichtung," *Deutsche Vierteljahrsschrift für Literaturwissenschaft und Geistesgeschichte*, 31 (1957), 465–505.

Morse, B. J. "The Fifth Duino Elegy: Commentary," *The Welsh Review*, 3 (1944), 125–29.

Müller, Paul E. "Rilkes Stellung zur Sprache: Interpretation von Sonett XV unter Zuhilfenahme der IX. Duineser Elegie," *Der Deutschunterricht*, 10 (1958), 39–44.

Murat, J. "Unité et dualité dans les 'Elégies de Duino' et les 'Sonnets à Orphée,' " *Etudes Germaniques*, 3 (1948), 319–27.

Parry, Idris. "Rilke and the Idea of *Umschlag*," *Modern Languages*, 39 (1958), 136–40.

Peters, H. F. *Rainer Maria Rilke: Masks and the Man*. Seattle: University of Washington Press, 1960.

Politzer, Heinz. "Some Aspects of 'Late Art' in Rainer Maria Rilke's Fifth Duino Elegy," *Germanic Review*, 32 (1957), 282–98.

Pickle, Linda S. "The Balance of Sound and Silence in the *Duineser Elegien* and *Sonette an Orpheus*," *Journal of English and Germanic Philology*, 70 (1971), 583–99.

Pongs, Hermann. "Rilkes Umschlag und das Erlebnis der Frontgeneration," *Dichtung und Volkstum*, 37 (1936), 75–97.

———. "Zum ersten Entwurf der Zehnten Elegie," *Dichtung und Volkstum*, 37 (1936), 97–99.

Prang, Helmut. "Der moderne Dichter und das arme Wort," *Germanisch-Romanische Monatsschrift*, 38 (1957), 130–45.

Purtscher-Wydenbruck, Nora. *Rilke, Man and Poet*. London: Lehmann, 1949.

Reichart, W. A. "Rilke's Fifth *Duino Elegy* and Picasso's *Les Saltimbanques*," *Modern Language Notes*, 61 (1946), 279–81.

Rickman, H. P. "Poetry and the Ephemeral: Rilke's and Eliot's Conceptions of the Poet's Task," *German Life and Letters, N. S.*, 12 (1958/59), 174–85.

Ritzer, Walter. *Rainer Maria Rilke Bibliographie*. Vienna: O. Kerry, 1951.

Ruprecht, Erich. "Rilkes Botschaft in den Duineser Elegien." *Die Botschaft der Dichter*. Stuttgart: Schmiedel, 1947, pp. 335–372.

Salis, J. P. von. *Rainer Maria Rilke. The Years in Switzerland*. Translated by N. K. Cruickshank. London: Hogarth Press, 1964.

Schäfer, Otto. "Die Duineser Elegien Rainer Maria Rilkes," *Germanisch-Romanische Monatsschrift*, 24 (1936), 343–58.

Schelbitzki, Linda L. "Rilke's Poetic Vocabulary in the *Duineser Elegien* and *Sonette an Orpheus*," (Colorado, 1969) *Dissertation Abstracts International*, 31 (1970/71): 398A.

Schleiner, Louise. "The Angel and the Necessary Angel: Formalist Readings of Rilke and Stevens," *Literatur in Wissenschaft und Unterricht*, 2 (1969), 215–37.

Schlötermann, Heinz. *Rainer Maria Rilke: Versuch einer Wesensdeutung*. Munich: Reinhardt, 1966.

Schmidt-Pauli, Elisabeth von. *Hiersein ist herrlich: Erläuterungen zu Rainer Maria Rilkes Duineser Elegien*. Konstanz: Nußdorf Internationaler Verlag, 1948.

Schroeder, Adolf E. "R. M. Rilke in America: A Bibliography, 1926–1951," *Monatshefte*, 44 (1952), 27–38.

Schwerte, Hans. "Das Lächeln in den Duineser Elegien," *Germanisch-Romanische Monatsschrift, N. S.*, 4 (1954), 289–98.

Seyppel, Joachim. "The 'Deadly Angel' in R. M. Rilke's Second Elegy," *Philological Quarterly*, 37 (1958), 18–25.

Sheppard, Richard, "From the 'Neue Gedichte' to the 'Duineser Elegien': Rilke's Chandos Crisis," *Modern Language Review*, 68 (1973), 577–92.

———. "Rilke's 'Duineser Elegien'—A Critical Appreciation in the Light of Eliot's 'Four Quartets,' " *German Life and Letters*, N. S., 20 (1966/67), 205–17.

Siebels, Eva. "Rilke und Kassner: Ein Versuch," *Dichtung und Volkstum*, 37 (1936), 22–35.

Spender, Stephen. "Rilke and the Angels, Eliot and the Shrines." *The Creative Element*. London: Hamish Hamilton, 1953, pp. 56–76.

Stahl, E. L. *Creativity: A Theme from 'Faust' and the 'Duino Elegies.'* Oxford: Clarendon Press, 1961.

———. "The Duineser Elegien." *Rainer Maria Rilke. Aspects of his Mind and Poetry*. Ed. William Rose and G. Craig Houston. London: Sidgwick and Jackson, 1938, pp. 123–71.

———. "Introduction." *Rainer Maria Rilke's Duineser Elegien*. Oxford: Basil Blackwell, 1965, pp. ix–xxxvii.

Steffensen, Steffen. "Rainer Maria Rilke: Les Elégies de Duino. Genèse et interpretation," *Etudes Germaniques*, 1 (1946), 416–27.

Stein, Jack M. "The Duino Elegies," *Germanic Review*, 27 (1952), 272–79.

Steiner, Jacob. "Das Motiv der Puppe bei Rilke." *Kleists Aufsatz über das Marionettentheater: Studien und Interpretationen*. Ed. Helmut Sembdner. Berlin: Schmidt, 1967, pp. 132–70.

———. *Rilkes Duineser Elegien*. Bern and Munich: Francke, 1962.

Stephens, Anthony. " 'Puppenseele' und 'Weltinnenraum,' " *Seminar*, 6 (1970), 63–75.

———. "Rilke's Essay *Puppen* and the Problem of the Divided Self," *German Life and Letters*, N. S. 22 (1968/69), 302–15.

Stockum, Th. C. van. "Der gedankliche Hintergrund von Rilkes Duineser Elegien," *Neophilologus*, 32 (1948), 109–21.

Sugar, L. de. "Le Voyage en Egypte de R. M. Rilke, d'aprés ses lettres." *Folklore Studies in Honor of Arthur Palmer Hudson*. Chapel Hill: North Carolina Folklore Society, 1965.

Theißen, Mien. "Zum Grundgedanken vom Auftrag der Erde," *Dichtung und Volkstum*, 37 (1936), 66–75.

Thiekötter, Friedel. *Die Negation im Werk Rilkes*. Münster: Selbstverlag, 1971.

Thurn und Taxis-Hohenlohe, Fürstin Marie von. *Erinnerungen an Rainer Maria Rilke*. 2nd ed. Frankfurt am Main: Insel, 1966.

―――. *Memoirs of a Princess*. Translated by Nora Purtscher-Wydenbruck. London: Hogarth Press, 1959.

Trapp, Arnold. *R. M. Rilkes Duineser Elegien*. Gießen: von Münchowsche Universitätsdruckerei, 1936.

Vietta, Egon. "Über die Duineser Elegien," *Die neue Rundschau*, 47 (1936), 1306–18.

Waas, J. B. *Über ein unbekanntes Fragment der Zehnten Duineser Elegie von Rainer Maria Rilke*. Minden: Ising, 1950.

Wahr, Fred B. " 'Der Magier' as an Interpretation of Rilke's Later Thought," *Journal of English and Germanic Philology*, 46 (1947), 188–98.

Weigand, Elsie. "Rilke and Eliot: The Articulation of the Mystic Experience. A Discussion Centering on the Eighth Duino Elegy and Burnt Norton," *Germanic Review*, 30 (1955), 198–210.

Weigand, Hermann J. "The Poet's Dilemma: An Interpretation of Rilke's Second *Duino Elegy*," *Publications of the Modern Language Association of America*, 82 (1967), 3–13.

Wirl, Julius. "Englische Übertragungen von Rilkes erster Duineser Elegie." *Oesterreich und die angelsächsische Welt*. Ed. O. Hietsch. Vienna: Braumüller, 1961, pp. 432–53.

Wocke, Helmut. "Rilkes Duineser Elegien," *Germanisch-Romanische Monatsschrift*, 20 (1932), 333–50.

―――. "Rilkes Welthaltung in den Duineser Elegien: Grundsätzliches zur Frage der wissenschaftlichen Interpretation," *Zeitschrift für Ästhetik und allgemeine Kunstwissenschaft*, 37 (1943), 32–41.

Wodtke, Friedrich Wilhelm. "Das Problem der Sprache beim späten Rilke," *Orbis Litterarum*, 11 (1956), 64–109.

Wolf, Werner. "Rainer Maria Rilke und die Liebenden," *Acta Academiae Aboensis*, 18 (1949), 333–58.

————. *Rainer Maria Rilkes Duineser Elegien. Eine Textdeutung.* Heidelberg: Winter, 1937.

Wood, Frank H. "Rilke and Eliot," *Germanic Review*, 27 (1952), 246–59.

————. "Rilke and the Theater," *Monatshefte*, 43 (1951), 15–26.

————. *Rainer Maria Rilke: The Ring of Forms.* Minneapolis: University of Minnesota Press, 1958.

Wunderlich, Eva C. "R. M. Rilkes religiöse Ideen," *German Quarterly*, 21 (1948), 185–95.

# UNIVERSITY OF NORTH CAROLINA
## STUDIES IN THE GERMANIC LANGUAGES
## AND LITERATURES

*Initiated by* RICHARD JENTE (1949–1952), *established by* F. E. COENEN (1952–1968)

### Publication Committee

SIEGFRIED MEWS, EDITOR       JOHN G. KUNSTMANN       GEORGE S. LANE

HERBERT W. REICHERT       CHRISTOPH E. SCHWEITZER       SIDNEY R. SMITH

*For other volumes in the "Studies" see page ii and following pages.*

**Send orders to: (U.S. and Canada)**
**The University of North Carolina Press, P.O. Box 2288**
**Chapel Hill, N.C. 27514**
**(All other countries) Feffer and Simons, Inc., 31 Union Square, New York, N.Y. 10003**

# UNIVERSITY OF NORTH CAROLINA
## STUDIES IN THE GERMANIC LANGUAGES
## AND LITERATURES

*Initiated by* RICHARD JENTE (1949–1952), *established by* F. E. COENEN (1952–1968)

### Publication Committee

*For other volumes in the "Studies" see preceding and following pages and p. ii.*

# UNIVERSITY OF NORTH CAROLINA
## STUDIES IN THE GERMANIC LANGUAGES
## AND LITERATURES

*Initiated by* RICHARD JENTE (1949–1952), *established by* F. E. COENEN (1952–1968)

### Publication Committee

SIEGFRIED MEWS, EDITOR    JOHN G. KUNSTMANN    GEORGE S. LANE

HERBERT W. REICHERT    CHRISTOPH E. SCHWEITZER    SIDNEY R. SMITH

*For other volumes in the "Studies" see preceding pages and p. ii*

**Order reprinted books from: AMS PRESS, Inc.,**
**56 East 13th Street, New York, N.Y. 10003**